There is no question that today's college student is different. They see life differently; their needs are different; the world they live in is different. In *Worlds Apart*, Chuck Bomar, one of the leading experts on college students, gives us a solid, clear, and empowering resource for coming alongside these emerging adults. When I want to learn about college students, I read Chuck Bomar.

Chap Clark, PhD
Author of *Hurt 2.0: Inside the World of Today's Teenagers*
Professor of Youth, Family, and Culture at Fuller Theological Seminary

Chuck Bomar gives very keen insight into the minds and hearts of what often can be a confusing generation to understand. Chuck writes not just out of his research and experience but out of passion, love, and belief in this generation.

Dan Kimball
Author of *They Like Jesus But Not the Church*

Personally, as the father of three adolescents, this book was an important and relevant read for me. Professionally, as the president of an evangelistic ministry, this book was an essential and strategic read. Eighteen- to twenty-five-year-olds are the future of our communities, our churches, and ultimately, our world. We need to invest in them if we are to invest in a brighter future. Chuck Bomar shows us how.

Kevin Palau
President, Luis Palau Association

Making a difference in the lives of today's college students requires us to rethink how we approach our relationships with them. In *Worlds Apart*, Chuck Bomar gives us deep perspective from the front lines of ministry. Wondering what your college students might be thinking right now? Chuck can tell you.

Reggie Joiner
Founder and CEO of Orange

D1244948

We—the church—haven't had a clue how to connect with college-age students for a long time. Peek inside an average church and it shows. Before we race off to construct lame programs and structures that miss the mark, we could all benefit from increased understanding. Thankfully, Chuck Bomar has arrived with this book that offers just that.

Mark Oestreicher
The Youth Cartel

If you work with students, or have or struggled to understand the next generation in any way, read this book! In *Worlds Apart*, Chuck combines a pastor's heart with cutting-edge research in a way that will help you lead your church and your family.

Jared Herd
Author of *More Lost Than Found*

Chuck Bomar is refreshingly clear on how all of us, regardless of our age or stage in life, can build authentic relationships with younger adults. You'll not only love what Chuck has to say, you'll love how what he has to say will impact your life.

Carey Nieuwhof
Coauthor of *Parenting Beyond Your Capacity*
Lead Pastor of Connexus Community Church, Toronto

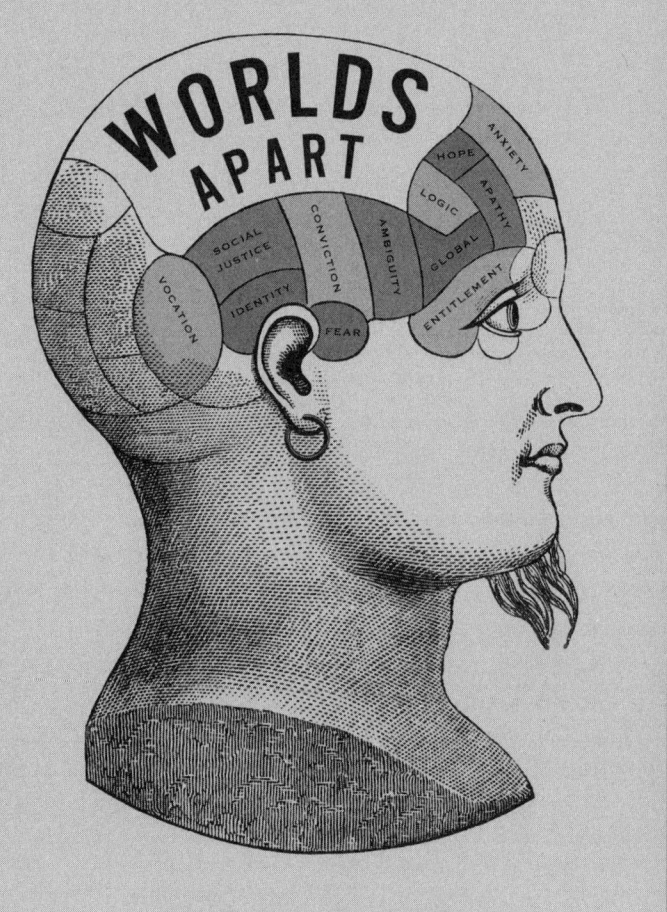

[*Understanding the Mindset and Values of 18–25 Year Olds*]

WORLDS APART

CHUCK BOMAR

AUTHOR OF *COLLEGE MINISTRY FROM SCRATCH*

youth
specialties

ZONDERVAN.com/
AUTHORTRACKER
follow your favorite authors

ZONDERVAN

Worlds Apart: Understanding the Mindset and Values of 18-25 Year Olds
Copyright © 2011 by Chuck Bomar

This title is also available as a Zondervan ebook.
Visit www.zondervan.com/ebooks.

This title is also available in a Zondervan audio edition.
Visit www.zondervan.fm.

Requests for information should be addressed to:

Zondervan, Grand Rapids, Michigan 49530

ISBN: 978-0-310-67106-0

Cover design: David Carlson, Gearbox
Cover illustration: Fotosearch
Interior design: David Conn

Printed in the United States of America

11 12 13 14 15 16 /DCI/ 23 22 21 20 19 18 17 16 15 14 13 12 11 10 9 8 7 6 5 4 3 2 1

CONTENTS

ACKNOWLEDGMENTS

I want to thank all the parents who offered their insight into this project. I understand why you wish to remain anonymous, but you are not to me. I am extremely grateful for the time each of you has spent reading unedited chapters and taking evenings, Saturday afternoons, or late-night phone calls to discuss this material.

I want to thank the elders of Colossae Church. Thank you for your patience with my often too-big-picture mind. I don't thank you enough for your support of me as a person and of the ministry I feel called to outside of our church. But my relationship with you has meant more than you probably know—and more than I probably let on most of the time.

This book would clearly not be possible if it weren't for my wife, Barbara. Thank you for your love and support as I have lain awake at night restlessly writing down thoughts—or snoring out of exhaustion from only two hours of sleep the previous night. I love being on mission with you.

Last, but certainly not least, I want to acknowledge both my girls, Karis and Hope. I love you so much. As I write this I'm looking forward to playing Crazy Eights with you tonight! (Note to reader: I have a deal with my girls to make sure their names are in every book I write. I am thankful for them, for sure, but this is also to make sure I don't get in trouble when the first copies arrive at my door!)

BY CHUCK BOMAR

INTRODUCTION

I love college-age people. And I'm blessed to be around so many. I thoroughly enjoy spending time with them. I love learning about their lives, and I am constantly blessed by learning *from* them. I guess what I'm trying to say here is not only do I have quality friendships and a deep love for individuals in this stage of life, but also for this younger generation as a whole.

I hope you can say the same. If not, I hope this book will move you in that direction as I share with you some of what I've learned through my relationships with this age group.

If I'm honest, I find that people of older generations are often bewildered by people in the eighteen- to twenty-five-year-old range. It's easy for those of us with more years behind us to criticize younger generations rather than to walk lovingly alongside them. I believe this is mostly due to a lack of understanding and perspective—and it's a loss for both sides. College-age people need people like you in their lives. They are at a launching point on their life trajectory and desperately need (and desire) someone to help them navigate their world. However, I'd also suggest you could use these younger people to be a part of your life as well!

The problem is every generation has grown up in a different world. That leaves different generations living worlds apart from one another today. The desire to bridge that gap is what led me to write this book. I want to play a role in bringing your world together with a younger person's. You might be a parent or leader of young people. You may feel bewildered by, frustrated with, or simply interested in college-age people. Whatever the case, this book is for you.

Maybe you're a parent at the end of your emotional rope and searching for practical advice. You might be a leader who is desperate for insight into the minds of college-age people. Or perhaps you're simply desiring to gain perspective and deeper understanding into what is actually happening in the lives of people between the ages of eighteen and twenty-five. If any of that describes you, this book is written for you.

The college-age years are a complex stage of life. I believe they are also the most catalytic stage of life and one packed with unlimited potential. My hope is that as you increase your understanding of this life stage, you'll gain fresh perspective on what the people in it think about, how they develop their identities, and how their values drive their decisions. And all of this will hopefully lead you to a loving posture as you seek to bring your world closer to a college-age person's.

It's inevitable that generational values will vary. We all look at the generations on either side of us and recognize differences. But in order to bring our worlds together we must recognize the common ground we have while patiently operating with our differences in mind. This book will not only articulate the differences you may have with today's college-age generation, but will help you navigate them practically too.

I have broken down and simplified what seem to be some of the biggest tensions that disconnect different generations in the home, on campuses, and in churches. In order to help you navigate these areas, we must begin by gaining perspective of the college-age world, what has shaped the way college-age individuals think about certain things, and when they begin thinking about them.

I'll begin by giving a brief glimpse into the ways the world of today's young people differs from the world you likely grew up in. We'll learn how to operate with those differences in mind and how to find common ground. From there the book will take you on a journey toward clarity, understanding, and fresh perspective on living together and loving well even when our generations seem far apart.

So, with that, let's begin. . . .

CHAPTER 1

WHO EXACTLY ARE WE TALKING ABOUT?

I work from coffee shops a lot, and there is one thing I know to be true: Overhearing other people's conversations is unavoidable. Some conversations are no big deal, and some just make you laugh. But others, well, you wish you never knew about.

I was recently having coffee with a college freshman named Katy. She had been coming to our church for about a month, and she simply wanted to learn more about who we are, what we do, and why we're going about things the way we are. She warned me she had a lot of questions, so we ordered our java and I told her I was more than happy to try to answer.

Sitting at the table closest to Katy and I were two women and two men that I would guess were in their mid-sixties. They were solving all the world's problems. They had answers and opinions on every political move in history and things they thought politicians should have moved on. The topic of President Bill Clinton's impeachment came up, and they were, of course, discussing everything from what they thought should have happened, to how things could have been handled better, to what his marriage is probably like today. They had it all figured out! It was quite fascinating eavesdropping material. And the volume at which they were talking made it impossible for us *not* to hear their conversation.

Despite the decibels projecting from the table three feet away from us, Katy and I were having our own great discussion about her life and her thoughts and questions regarding our church. Eventually, after all the world's problems were solved, the people at the table next to us left. I have to admit, I was a bit relieved. I could now focus on my conversation with Katy without being sidetracked.

But immediately after those folks left, Katy caught me by surprise. She looked at me and said, "So, wait, Bill Clinton was impeached? What was that all about?"

At first I was a bit shocked she didn't already know this, and frankly wondered if she was raised in a cave (okay, not really). I was caught off guard, but I was quickly reminded that the events surrounding President Clinton's impeachment all took place at the end of 1998, and Katy was only six or seven years old at the time. It would be quite alarming for a seven-year-old to have been fully aware of the situation and all its nuances. Know what I mean?

Anyway, I briefly explained the situation, and we moved on to our previous topics. We had a great conversation, I learned a lot about her, and she got most of her questions answered.

Katy might be an exception for younger people, and one might assume she would have at least learned about the presidential impeachment in school. But I would suggest she's not the only person her age who doesn't know all about the Clinton administration. I mean, can you imagine a seven-year-old today being able to understand anything about the controversy around President Obama's pursuit of medical reform? Of course not—it's not a part of their world. When the seven-year-olds of today get to college and overhear four people in a coffee shop reviewing Obama's presidency, they probably won't have a clue what's being talked about either.

It's conversations like this one with Katy that serve as abrupt reminders that so many of the world events that were a part of my life have in no way consciously influenced her or others her age.

And the opposite is also true. Kay has grown up in a very different world than the one I grew up in. The things that have shaped her development didn't necessarily shape me. As an adult I'm likely *aware* of the outside influences that have shaped her, but they haven't shaped me the way they've shaped her. And the things I've experienced as part of Generation X are often ancient history to her.

Conversations like this one with Katy make me realize we have grown up in two different worlds. They make me feel old sometimes! But those conversations can also cause me to wonder what I have in common with some of these younger people. It's not that we don't have anything in common—our faith could certainly be one of those commonalities, and we are actually similar in many other ways too. But the reality is our experiences—wars, technological advancements, economic depressions, demands in the workforce, worldview shaping movies, books, and government leaders—shape our perspectives. And perspective influences the way a generation thinks about life, including what each individual values, expects, and pursues as meaningful.

GROWING UP WITH DIFFERENT EXPECTATIONS

I remember going to a Starbucks for the first time and feeling out of place because I didn't know the appropriate lingo. I had no idea what to order, much less how to say it—was it *grand* or *grahn-day* or should I just skip the jargon and say large? I was blown away at the new language being yelled out so nonchalantly from behind the counter. Today I can rattle off the coffee shop lingo with the best of them—especially now living in Portland and working from coffee shops! But I remember when it was new. College-age people, however, have never known life without a barista. An occupation and terminology that was once reserved for coffee connoisseurs has always been part of their everyday life.

Coffee's central role in life probably hasn't greatly changed the way we think nor has it hugely impacted our values. But there are other things that have. Technology is one of them. This book is clearly not about technology, but I'd like to take you on a brief journey down memory lane just to illustrate how technology has created a different world to grow up in.

I own and frankly enjoy technologically advanced things. I view them as luxuries because they were things I never had growing up. College-age people, however, have never lived in a world without a total reliance on technology to function in a workplace, relationship, school, and even family life. My luxury has become their world's necessity. And it has created a very different world to grow up in. Technology is not the only thing that has changed our world, but it has changed at least two things in our everyday practical lives: What we expect and the way information is obtained. We may often see the technology-driven world we live in as a challenge, but it's not bad. And recognizing the differences can help us make the most of it. Just for fun, jump back with me a few years . . .

TECHNOLOGY IMPACTS EXPECTATIONS

It might be weird to think about, but all a college freshman knows is *digital* devices. You know, the kind that never skip! Remember when the Walkman was cutting edge? I mean, we could go for a run and not have to carry our boom box! And when the Discman came out we were totally beside ourselves—now we could listen to CDs in our car. We would drive down the street with our new CD holder hanging from our visor and excited to have a cord connecting our Discman to our car's cassette player. We were thankful for the sound quality and the immediate satisfaction of selecting the song we wanted without having to fast forward or rewind for a half hour.

Most college-age people have literally never owned, or possibly held, a cassette tape. When we mention having 45s, they think we're talking about guns. And you can forget about an eight-track cartridge! Man, I remember pulling those things out of the glove box and heaving them over to the center console. For people in college today everything has been available at the touch of a screen. They can carry more than 10,000 songs in a device that has no mechanical parts and is smaller than a cassette tape ever dreamed of being. Today's young adults are used to listening to what they want, when they want, anywhere they want—and on whatever device they have at that particular time.

In the college-age experience, VHS has never existed, and BETA is now a techie term used to describe the beginning stages of web-based development.

The computer with 1GB of memory is useless. "We will never need more than that," we used to say. But today's high quality cameras and cell phones that shoot HD video have made 1GB obsolete. College-age people expect nothing less than a 16GB device that can upload video for the entire world to see instantaneously—and that fits in a pocket.

I remember the Commodore 64. It was far from portable because the screen weighed about twenty pounds. I thought it was so cool, the black screen with green letters and all. And the keyboard—wow, you didn't have to push the button down a mile as if on a typewriter before the letter appeared! If current college-age people have ever seen a typewriter, it's probably been on a big-screen depiction of a World War II newsroom.

The only time they've gotten off the couch to change the channel is when a sibling wouldn't hand over the remote. Remember getting up to turn the knob on the television? I had channels two through thirteen, four of which didn't work, and I was super-excited when that was doubled so that we could flip from A to B channels. (Wow, unfortunately for me, that sounds far too similar to "I used to walk to school uphill both ways.") College-age people today have never known less than hundreds of channels they can choose from and shows they can watch on demand and pause when they have to use the restroom. Of course, they still feel like they have nothing to watch.

For better or worse the expectations they have grown up with are simply different than what I and probably you grew up with. Their consistent experience of top quality and instantaneous *everything* has molded the way they think and what they have come to expect. Technological developments are inevitable. Like me, you probably enjoy much of what technology brings and have developed some of the same technological dependencies and expectations as young people. But the difference is that you didn't grow up being shaped by them. Your technology has been add-ons, not core building blocks. The same technologies have shaped who college-age people are and how they think.

I'm assuming that's not as shocking as the first time you learned Santa Claus doesn't actually fly around in a sled pulled by reindeer. You *know* something is different. We can laugh at the differences when we see them in print, but the question is do we take them to heart as we seek to relate to college-age people?

TECHNOLOGY IMPACTS THE FLOW OF INFORMATION

The impact of technology doesn't stop with entertainment. Perhaps the bigger and more central effects can be seen in how information is obtained. Do you remember someone knocking on your door trying to sell encyclopedias? Yeah, well, most college-age people have never even picked one up. Those are in the section of the library many are no longer required to go into. The idea of having to go to a library, pull out index cards to see where to begin looking, pull a book off the shelf, and then look through it alphabetically to find an answer is completely ridiculous.

Searching directly and instantaneously for information has always been the expectation for college-age people. And they don't even know that Al Gore created the Internet. (Come on, you can laugh at that!) All joking aside, they've never known life without the Internet. If they want to start a business, they create and promote a website before thinking about registering the business.

They would never think of calling the Yellow Pages to place an ad for their business because they are far too environmentally conscious to do that. What a total waste of time and a tree!

To fill out a time sheet by hand is as archaic as Moses chipping away at a stone. And they certainly can't believe that developing and printing business forms used to be a thriving enterprise. Young adults expect to be able to get information out to the world by the use of a touch pad or screen.

How about a home phone? Nah, that's stupid. Why would anyone ever get one of those? Only old people have landlines. They are viewed as a total waste of money. We're talking about a generation that has always been available, expects everyone else to always be available, and can never seem to disconnect. Writing in cursive might as well be Paleo-Hebrew because college-age people don't use it anymore. They may handwrite in their journal, but would never dream of writing an entire paper by hand. Having to print out an essay or research paper to hand in at the beginning of class is even fading. It's now normal to email it to the professor by 11:59 p.m. on the due date. That is far more efficient and environmentally conscious.

The Moose Lodge is considered to be either a ski resort or a cult. Paying money to be a part of a social club is insane, especially when you can have a voice into any subject online and can be immediately connected to thousands of people's lives and thoughts from an iPad that connects to wireless networks for free. They expect things to revolve around them and their timing.

Before we go any farther, we need to be careful. We can't arrogantly point the finger at "them" and "their" self-centered ways of life. The truth is we also have many of the same tendencies. Ours may show up in different ways, but it's not like our generations were known for their selflessness. Actually, if you look closely at this generation of college-age people, you'll find that they seem to be more concerned about other people than any

American generation that has gone before them. They are overall compassionate and believe they can make a difference.

As you grew up you probably watched television news, listened to the radio, or read newspapers in order to get a glimpse into international affairs and events—if you were even interested in something happening so far away. Today it doesn't matter if you're interested or not because CNN's Twitter updates are retweeted by your friends on Facebook. It's hard not to be aware of what is happening in the world at any given moment.

Perhaps the biggest impact of growing up in a world where you always have information at your fingertips is that the world seems much smaller for younger generations. This has played a huge role in their desire and interest to be involved in world affairs and social justice work worldwide. If there are riots in Uganda, they don't need to watch the news because they likely got a text message notifying them of a friend's Facebook status that included a link to a LiveStream video of what is happening. No need for a major network camera crew; everyone has cell phones that can upload video immediately. The world for us used to seem huge, and we never expected to be up on things on the other side of the planet. The world of the college-age childhood is much smaller. The other side of the world is in the palm of their hand.

My point is not to say the world in which this younger generation has grown up is better or worse than the one you did. However, it is important to realize that they are in fact different. We have grown up in a world that has grounded us in certain perspectives and practices, and we have been exposed to circumstances and world events that have impacted the way we think and what we expect. College-age people are grounded in some of the same cultural perspectives as we are, but there are distinct differences too. And that's what this book is about.

As small and humorous as some of these generational differences may seem, they nevertheless should impact how we relate to younger people.

GENERATION TO GENERATION

So what are we to do with all these generational differences? I could go on writing pages and pages of differences and still only scratch the surface of outside influences that make every age stage today different from the same age stage in another generation. It's helpful to identify such influences and differences. It's key to remember and consider them as we intentionally pursue relationships with college-age people. If we don't, we will inevitably place unrealistic expectations on young people, get frustrated, and continue widening the gap between our worlds.

I constantly talk to parents who don't feel like they can relate to their kids. They are totally bewildered and confused when trying to figure out what their child wants and needs from them. I speak with church leaders across the country who are also at a loss, frustrated because twentysomethings "just never seem to grow up." Many, both parents and church leaders, simply throw their hands up in hopeless surrender and stop trying to figure it all out.

My hope is to bring some clarity, connection, and common ground between you and this generation widely known as the Millennials. The Millennial label is fine in referring to people who have graduated from high school in the new millennium. It's a good term, but it's not very descriptive. So to be a little more pointed I usually refer to this generation of younger people as Generation Higher Ed. I coined this term because I believe the pressures that higher education has brought into our world have affected this generation far more than most think. As we've seen, technology and other aspects of our culture certainly play a part in shaping them too, but the need for more education has been affecting the way we think about our lives for more than a hundred years. We are now seeing this play out in a number of interesting ways. And this is exactly what the next chapter will begin showing you.

CHAPTER 2

GENERATION HIGHER ED–
A NEW CONTEXT

For much more than a decade now I have been processing some questions regarding college-age life:

- What has influenced the changes in thinking and lifestyle for this younger generation?

- What do these things mean for us older adults?

- What exactly are the differences between generations?

- How can two generations of people that have been shaped and molded by different things come together?

- And how can people of older generations, such as parents, bridge the differences and connect with college-age people?

Before we begin to answer these questions, let's first make sure we're in touch with the reality of our context.

A NEW AGE STAGE

As one generation gets older another follows, and in that shift the values, expectations, pressures, and pursuits of its people continually evolve. This evolution occurs because the world one generation grew up in was different than the previous generation's. People in the generations that follow you are entering life stages you have long since passed. But in all reality it's a different age stage. They might be the same age as you once were, but the times have created a different world for those in that stage. And this causes their lives to look different than ours did when we were that age. For example, today's childhood is drastically different from your childhood.

We find ourselves in a time sociologists are referring to as "the changing timetable for adulthood." Historically sociologists have said that the transition to adulthood is made after:

1. finishing school

2. moving out of the home

3. being financially independent

4. getting married

5. having a child

When all five benchmarks are passed, sociologists suggest a person has officially entered adult life. It's interesting to note that in 1960, 77 percent of women and 65 percent of men had passed all these milestones by the time they were 30 years old. By 2000 these numbers had dropped to less than half of women and only 33 percent for men.[1] The trend continues today and has been a popular media topic. In 2010 the *New York Times* printed articles such as "Long Road to Adulthood Is Growing Even Longer" and "What Is It About 20-Somethings?"

We can take a brief step back, look at the trajectory of this trend, and see that a pretty significant shift has occurred over the years. The research shows that the transition into adulthood is later in life than ever before, and this has brought us to a pivotal moment in history. We now have a new stage of life that has never existed before: a pre-adult or late-adolescent stage.

Adolescence is understood as a time of inconsistency, which is largely due to it being a time where people are trying to figure out who they are and how they fit into society. *Adolescent* is not a derogatory term in my mind. It's simply a term used to describe someone who is in between dependent childhood and independent adulthood. Sociologist Erik Erikson is the one who helped define this by labeling adolescence as the time of exploring identity, discovering who you are, and finding your role in society. He spoke of "prolonged adolescence" (or extended adolescence) being typical of industrialized cultures, such as the United States. He describes this state of later adolescence (typically known as the seventeen to twenty-five age range today) as a time of "free role experimentation" where people are trying to figure out who they are and find "a niche in some section of society."[2] This later adolescent stage, which I also call the *college-age stage* of life or *twenty-somethings* is a time of searching, exploration, and discovery of self and how one fits in society. (I just can't use the same wording all the time otherwise my editors get on me for repetition.)

If there is any age group of people trying to find a niche or place in society today, it's college-age people. This stage of life can be a time of clarity, but universally it's also one of confusion. I point this out because missing this fact causes us older adults to either place unrealistic expectations on college-age people or miss what they need from us parents, school administrators, church leaders, or employers. And instead of missing it, I'd like to help you nail it.

My friend Chap Clark in his book *Hurt* has articulated this definition:

> Adolescence, then, is a psychosocial, independent search for a unique identity or separateness, with the end goals being a certain knowledge of who one is in relation to others, a willingness to take responsibility for who one is becoming, and a realized commitment to live with others in community. Basically adolescence is a time of becoming self aware and beginning to think about how they might contribute to society.[3]

The college-age years match this definition. They are clearly a time of late adolescent exploration and searching. They are no longer a settled down, consistent adultlike time of life. I know this can be irritating at times to watch because it's likely different than what you experienced at the same age, but this is the reality we face.

You've probably noticed the difference too. You may not have worded it exactly the same way, but you've experienced that twentysomethings today think about adult life completely different than previous generations did at the same age. And they think about it at a different time in life, too. It wasn't long ago that someone could graduate from high school, get a decent paying job, move out, become independent, support a family, and thus enter adult life. But this isn't the case anymore. It's time to adjust our thinking.

Previous generations can easily view today's college-age folks as irresponsible. "Those twentysomethings" can't seem to land. They're lost, aimless, have very little initiative. They are lazy, afraid of hard work, or even have a fear of commitment. These descriptions can certainly apply to some individuals— but it's definitely not an accurate assessment that applies across the board. In fact many people in their twenties are ambitious and very successful by any generational standard. We have to be careful to avoid overgeneralizing. And even where these negative characteristics do apply, we must avoid the negative labels and look for the reasons behind them. The bottom line is adult living and thinking is getting more and more delayed in our culture due to factors well beyond the control of any individual college-age person.

Isn't it easy to wonder if this whole delayed adultlike thing (or prolonged adolescence) is simply delaying the inevitable and possibly allowing immaturity to thrive in our culture? Many are completely bewildered by and frustrated with those in this life stage, calling them "boys with beards" or using other clever phrases that suggest they're not as mature as they should be. They belittle the idea of singles playing video games and not stepping up to be "real men." And rightly so in many ways.

However, this type of talk going back and forth has developed little if any benefit for anyone, and can cause tempers to flair and generations to grow farther apart. It is precisely why I want to encourage us to gently step back, take a deep breath, and look at a few things before we overgeneralize and jump to wrong conclusions.

I'm not condoning a lazy and aimless life for anyone, nor am I an advocate of adolescence being a lifestyle. But we can talk about the differences between generations until we're blue in the face and still miss the point. We have to look carefully into what has caused these changes, starting with the progression of higher education in their world.

IN PURSUIT OF HIGHER EDUCATION

I suggest the biggest impacting factor changing the landscape of eighteen to twenty-five-year-old lives is the need for higher education. This is critical to understand if we are going to gain insight into this stage of life and understand their perspectives on values, meaning, success, and what they need from us.

I'm not much of a statistics person, but once I looked into it I was shocked with what I found happening with higher education. I knew the amount of people attending college was rising, but I had no idea how much, nor was I aware of the impact this was actually having on the mindset of current college-age people. Looking at some of these statistics and understanding why so many people are pursuing this level of education will provide a framework for understanding and applying the chapters that follow.

Between 1970 and 2009, the number of eighteen- to twenty-four-year-olds obtaining more education in degree-granting institutions increased by 97 percent.[4] In 1950 less than 10 percent of eighteen- to twenty-four-year-olds were continuing education (including high school enrollment), but in 2009 the amount obtaining some college education was almost 76 percent *without* including high school enrollment.[5] (See Figure 2.1).

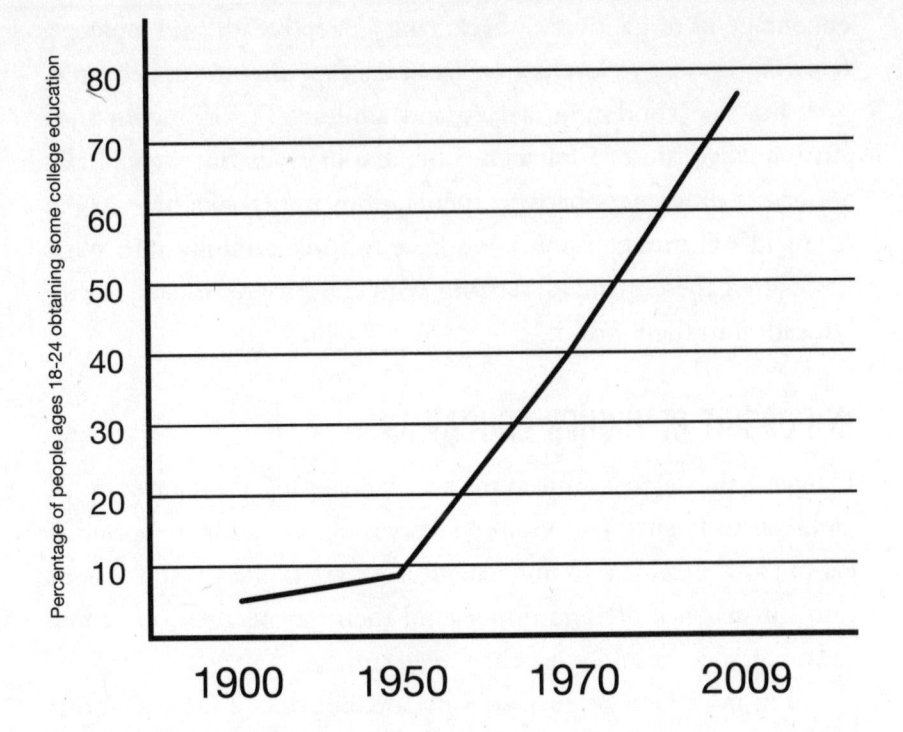

Percentage of people ages 18-24 obtaining some college education

1900 1950 1970 2009

Figure 2.1. People Pursuing College Education

In the 1950s some college-level education was of benefit. Today *some* doesn't really help at all. High school students recognize this. In fact the Bureau of Labor Statistics has reported that there were 2.9 million youths who graduated from high school between January and October of 2009 and 2.1 million of them were enrolled in college classes in October of 2009.[6] That leaves very few pursuing the sociological adulthood markers of getting a job, becoming independent, and starting a family. I think the necessity to further education before jumping into the workforce is probably the biggest factor contributing to delayed adulthood.

We know that the enrollment in degree-granting institutions continues to increase. Between 1997 and 2007, undergraduate enrollment increased at a rapid rate of 26 percent, moving from 14.5 million to 18.2 million. Much of this growth was in full-time enrollment. The number of full-time students rose 34 percent, while the number of part-time students rose 15 percent.[7]

Not only is the enrollment increasing, so is the amount of time it takes to complete an education. Approximately 57 percent of full-time, first-time bachelor's or equivalent degree-seekers attending four-year institutions took six years to complete a four-year degree.[8] It obviously takes even longer for part-timers or those who take some time off after graduating high school.[9]

Then there are those continuing on to pursue a master's level of education or greater. This number is growing as well. Graduate level education enrollment grew 60 percent between 1970 and 1980, stabilized during the 1980s and increased again by 18 percent between 1997 and 2007.[10]

My experience has been that some recent grads always planned on continuing with a master's level education, while others decide to because they simply don't know what else to do. One recent graduate has publicized her experience on a blog and provides a perfect example of this point.

After graduating, the state of the economy left this graduate "devoid of the normal graduation excitement" and instead she found herself to be a "scrambling worrywart." She found herself in an economy where she couldn't find a job to support herself, let alone one that allowed her to pursue her passions. So without an office desk to sit behind, she went back to a school desk, in the pursuit of more higher education. Her blog published by *USA Today* says:

> Many of us were studying and applying so we could continue receiving our benefits, delay student loan repayments, and buy more time to really figure out and pursue our passions. Although our approach appears misguided, although our debts will multiply exponentially, and although we are signing over more of our lives to academia, there is a certain comfort in sitting behind a desk, with a group of your peers, studying

something you like, and waiting for the chaos of the economy to subside together . . . and, maybe, just maybe, when we turn our next tassel, we will feel the pang of excitement as we set out into the world with purpose and pride.[11]

The evolution of higher education has our culture at a point where a master's degree is what a bachelor's degree used to be. With nowhere else to go, more and more people find themselves pursuing higher and higher education. And, as we will see in the next section, this familiar pattern has been taking place for more than 100 years.

In 2005 there were more 25- to 29-year-olds still in school (13 percent) than there were in the wider age range of 18- to 24-year-olds in 1950 (9 percent).[12] And the National Center for Education Statistics projects a continuing rise in the percentage of enrollment for twentysomethings. They report an increase of 13 percent of people older than 25 years old attending degree-granting institutions between 1995 and 2006, and expect it to increase by another 19 percent by 2017.[13]

This shift in the educational pursuits of our time has changed our culture and completely transformed the lives of 18- to 25-year-olds. It has

- drastically affected the way college-age people think about life.

- put off the milestones for transitioning into adulthood.

- changed the process of formulating an identity in society.

- created what some have called "adultolescence."

So let's briefly look at the development of this educational system to help better understand how we've gotten to this point and how it has impacted our culture. The development might surprise you a little, but it will help in understanding what's going on with the college-age people you know and love. Then we'll look at some long-term effects this has had on the college-age stage of life, the people in it, and their decisions and thought processes.

LABOR LAWS, THE GREAT DEPRESSION, AND EDUCATION

The only time we have seen an increase of enrollment in specific education levels like we see today was in the early 1900s. Once children were strong enough, they typically worked on the family farm or worked for others on a farm or in factories to earn income for their family. However, the turn of the twentieth century brought about the institution of labor laws limiting the amount children twelve years and under could work. This caused most children up to age twelve to begin attending public schools.

This might not seem like a big shift, but over time it changed the way children thought about life. It also changed the way children were viewed by society. They were no longer viewed as a means of helping financially support their families, but now were viewed as children needing the care and nurture of older adults. They thought like children because they no longer had to think about adult things like financially supporting themselves or a family. This change of view in culture can be identified by the fact that organizations including Boy Scouts (1910), Girl Scouts (1912) and 4-H (1902) developed and provided care and nurture for children outside of the home.

The majority of thirteen- to eighteen-year-olds were still at work farming, mining, or in factories because families simply couldn't lose the income nor could they imagine how more schooling would better their children's lives. Then the Great Depression hit in 1929 causing a major shift in the workforce, leaving many without work. Employers, if they could keep employees, kept the most experienced. This left the majority of teenagers without work.

While education funding initially took a hit, the Great Depression did bring about another huge influx of people into the education system and specifically in high school enrollment. Boston had the first public high school in 1820, but it wasn't until after the Depression hit that New York opened a high school. We don't normally think of it, but it wasn't that long ago that the idea of high school actually became a vital education level. Like younger children after labor laws were instituted, teens slowly began to think differently about life and were also viewed differently in society. Eventually the teenage years moved from being a time to engage in an adultlike working lifestyle to simply an additional necessary educational stage.

A new stage of adolescence referred to as mid-adolescence (generally high school age) began to be recognized and embraced. As more people were getting a high school education, competition began to rise in the job market. Once the Great Depression subsided, employers started hiring those with a high school diploma over those without, which created a demand for this educational level.

And this is an important point: Twelve-year-olds eventually stopped thinking about joining the workforce the following year because they knew they had to complete high school before pursuing a job. In other words, because the workforce was requiring more education, people in specific age stages began thinking about life differently and at later points in life.

This development of what we refer to as mid-adolescence didn't mean high school kids were dumb or matured slower than they used to. Rather, they were simply no longer *having to* think like an adult who was trying to help support a family. They were in a different stage of life now—an educational stage preparing for what was to come. Adults worked and thought about life issues. Kids went to school and thought about kids stuff.

Sound familiar?

It should because this is precisely what we're facing today with college level education. What we're seeing today has been developing for more than 100 years. Getting frustrated and bitter at twentysomethings who aren't settled into adult life could be related to getting frustrated with a sixteen-year-old for the same reason in 1942.

COLLEGE EXPECTATIONS CONTINUE CULTURAL SHIFT

There are many similarities between the past development of high school and the way college education has become necessary for the workforce. A huge jump in college enrollment took place in the late 1940s when World War II veterans returned to college and President Truman's administration made sweeping changes to higher education. Our present advances in technology and our results-oriented corporate systems are keeping people in school longer. Competition in the job market continues to raise enroll-ment. Higher unemployment rates due to economic hardship limit the number of available jobs, making a higher degree even more attractive. The likelihood of an employer hiring someone with a bachelor's degree over someone with only a high school diploma is extremely high.

High school students are feeling these pressures and now view high school graduation not as a rite of passage into adulthood, but simply a transition into the next stage of education. This leaves college-age people today thinking about adult life much like high school students did thirty-five years ago. The ages of eighteen to twenty-five are no longer a time of adult working life or thinking; they are a necessary educational stage that has led to an extension of adolescent thinking.

This educational development has drastically affected the path to adulthood. And it doesn't stop once students graduate from col-lege. The truth is a bachelor's degree is little if anything more than a high school diploma was thirty-five years ago. This has brought us to a point where people are still trying to figure out where they fit in society or what vocational path they'll follow even after graduating from college. It's a point some have called, "the morn-ing-after stage."

Yes, in ways college-age people are adults. Their thinking capacity is generally sharper than any previous stage of life; they are intuitive; and they have limitless potential. But when it comes to thinking about vocational direction, marriage, starting a family, and a variety of other things traditionally known as *adulthood*, college-age people are generally thinking as adolescents. The reality is the college-age years are a time of:

- transitions

- search for self and a unique fit into society

- reevaluation of all they grew up assuming was true

- search for meaning

- instability and inconsistency

- extreme egocentricism and priority on self-discovery

- loss of and search for belonging

The college-age years can no longer be referred to as adulthood. That means older generations need to adjust their expectations of people in this stage. I'm not suggesting that we move toward tolerating laziness or enabling aimless living. I am suggesting that we need to be careful how we view the people in this genera-tion. Even if eighteen- to twenty-five-year-olds are not enrolled in school, their thinking has largely been shaped by the educa-tional needs of their generation, which is quite different than yours probably was.

I've heard some advice given to college-age people over the years about how to grow up. I've heard all sorts of suggestions, such as:

- Drop all your lazy, unambitious friends.

- Read more to stimulate your brain.

- Write down your goals.

- Seek out a mentor.

- Just pick a direction and go with it.

While this advice may be well intentioned, it too easily comes across as shallow behavior management. It sounds insensitive, and it shows a lack of understanding of what *actually* is going on in the minds and culture of eighteen- to twenty-five-year-olds. We can do better. Before giving advice we need to look deeper at this higher education trend to understand the cultural differences and long-term implications higher education has placed on those in this stage.

In the next chapter we'll walk through four seemingly irreversible outcomes of the development of this educational system in the lives of college-age people today. We will then begin the journey of looking at specific issues this generation faces—understanding their mindsets and thought processes and comparing them with how previous generations typically think. The purpose is to give you insights into their minds and hearts and put you in their shoes, even for a moment. By understanding these things you will be able to see where some of the generational friction points are and how you can better build a bridge between your world and theirs.

CHAPTER 3

WANDERING IN THE LAND OF IN-BETWEEN

I have come across some interesting people while working with college-age people. Some are freakishly brilliant. And if I'm honest some are, well, just freakishly weird—or at least seem that way at first. Take Brian for instance. During Brian's freshman year at a local university, he used to come up to me every week and talk about the most off-the-wall things. One week his random topic was about a new Star Wars figure that came out. For some reason he was so excited to get it *and* explain every aspect of it to me.

This might be a somewhat normal conversation if we were having a cup of coffee and talking about new things coming out on the market. Even though I'm not a Star Wars fan and frankly would be bored stiff by the conversation, I'd be more than happy to discuss this new life-changing action figure because of Brian's interest. But this particular Star Wars conversation wasn't in the discuss-interesting-things-over-a-cup-of-coffee context. Instead, as he did every week for about a year, he came up immediately after I finished teaching a message at our college-age church service. It was in these somber and reflective moments that he somehow found it most appropriate to discuss things like the newest plastic robot.

After my first few encounters like this with Brian, I honestly thought he suffered from some sort of mental illness. The topics of our conversations were just too weird, too out of context, and off the wall to be considered normal. Unfortunately, and shamefully,

I have to admit that over time I found myself trying to avoid him because he would just consume my time and I wanted to be able to talk to other people.

I wish I had been more patient with him. My impatient character flaw eventually slapped me in the face when I found out more about Brian's life.

When he was seven years old Brian's parents literally abandoned him on a street corner in a city they were visiting. Standing outside of a liquor store where he thought his parents would return after getting bread, he eventually realized they were not going to come back. Apparently they went out the back door, never to return, and selfishly left their seven-year-old boy alone on a street corner.

No, this isn't a Hollywood tearjerker or some heartwrenching novel. It's real. It actually happened to Brian at seven years old. I have a daughter about this age, and I can't imagine her being in that situation. Tears well up just thinking about it.

Left in a city he'd never been to, knowing nobody, and having no money, Brian began wandering the streets with tears streaming down his face looking for his mommy and daddy. Thankfully it wasn't too long after walking around the city blocks desperately looking for a glimpse of his parents that an adult saw him and tried to help him find his parents.

But they were long gone.

From what I was told, Brian's parents had lost touch with all their family members before he was born, so Brian knew of no connections or history to look into. Nothing. Brian was alone. He only knew his mommy and daddy, and now they were nowhere to be found.

The gracious lady that found Brian wandering on the street eventually called the police and after many days of searching for his parents and relatives eventually connected him with social services. From that point Brian found himself going back and forth between living in foster care and living on the streets.

After hearing this my seeking to avoid Brian quickly became me intentionally pursuing him. I began to go into our conversations with a totally different mentality and an entirely new set of expectations. I was much more patient. I wanted to listen to him and honestly looked forward to our times together. I loved hearing him talk about the things that excited him, those things that helped him get out of bed in the morning—even if it was a Star Wars figure. Understanding Brian's background brought me to a point where I met him where he was, joined him in what excited him, and walked alongside him as patiently and lovingly as I could as he sifted through his past and his dreams for the future.

My point is that understanding what had shaped Brian's life allowed me to patiently embrace his behaviors, struggles, and limitations in life. I know this is a bit of an extreme example from my own experience, but it illustrates so clearly the point of our conversation. If we only look at some of the behavioral and lifestyle tendencies of this new generation we can get confused, impatient, and annoyed. On the other hand, if we accept their process of growing as being different than ours and recognize the unique pressures and tensions we don't personally relate to, then we can view these young people with the patience and understanding necessary to walk them toward independence and maturity. In doing this we can better understand what they need from us. And that's quite possibly the most important step of all.

Brian mostly needed someone to listen, pursue, and value him. I believe the same is also generally true for college-age people.

NO CLEAR RITE OF PASSAGE

As we learned in the last chapter, the timing of adultlike thinking has been greatly affected by the need for more education. Through this understanding my hope is that we can now look with new patience at some of the behavioral implications this has had in our culture and align our expectations realistically. The remainder of this chapter will walk through four irreversible ways higher education has impacted life after high school—and in many cases throughout the twentysomething years.

I always looked forward to being eighteen. When I was growing up eighteen was a sort of a rite of passage into adulthood when I would have the freedom to make my own choices and "do whatever I wanted." Oh how I longed for that birthday to come! In some ways I think my mom looked forward to this time as much as I did. It was going to be a point of relief for both of us, I think. Some of this stemmed from the fact that this marked the point when my parents would no longer be held personally accountable for my behaviors.

But I also think there was more to it. Much more, in fact.

In my parents' generation, and in ways mine as well, the rite of passage into adulthood was graduating from high school. In my parents' generation, those who went on to college were typically more financially well-off or abnormally ambitious. So college had very little, if anything, to do with our cultural view of exiting your parents' supervision and entering adulthood. Of course it varied to some degree, but generally speaking finishing high school was the rite of passage to being on your own.

Today is similar in that high school graduation is still a rite of passage, but different in that it's not into adulthood. Rather, it's now become the rite of passage to *begin* thinking about what you're going to do with your life. It's a space between two worlds. It's an educational preparatory stage for what's to come, but there's no real sense of what that might be or when it will come. And this can be a tough place to be.

With no clear rite of passage into adulthood, today's college-age people find themselves wandering in a space in between. College-age people know they need to work toward adulthood and certainly feel pressure to get there, but are unsure of what exactly this is supposed to look like. This creates confusion, stress, and an array of feelings and emotions that older generations have a hard time deciphering.

It can be a huge tension point for parents and their children. Watching their child go through an array of emotions and decisions along with a lack of commitment or communication, parents are left in a world of intellectual gymnastics trying to figure out what they're supposed to do or say. The relationships in this stage are no longer well defined, with independence and dependence pulling against each other. It can be a confusing and frustrating space for everyone involved.

College-age people have high hopes of finding a place in society through the workplace, but most don't know what they want to do yet.

Most assume at some point they will find a spouse to settle down with, but that's coming later and later in life.

Recent high school grads have left their high school identity, but haven't gained a sense of identity in the college world yet. And even when they do, they'll have to go through another identity crisis and search for self once they graduate from college.

College-age people are separating from their families, at least to some degree, and do so out of a search for who they are as individuals. But they are not yet truly independent from their parents, so they are constantly trying to figure out what and how much they should tell their parents about their process of self-discovery. In my experience I've seen them tell much less than parents would like. But parents shouldn't really expect to know about all the experiences that are now shaping their children into who they are becoming. Parents are used to knowing and solving the struggles their children face. But unlike many of the struggles of childhood, this is an internal struggle that can't be solved by parents. In fact, the active role of parents is often drastically reduced in the formation process at this age. It's a hard adjustment as a parent, but an important part of our children moving toward adulthood.

My point is the college-age years are clearly a time of internal instability where everything is up in the air and little is timely or organized. It's always been true that every person sifts through these issues differently and at different times, some with more clarity than others. But now in the midst of this search and pursuit of adulthood, the finish line has been blurred.

Some would like to think graduating from college and beginning a career is the new rite of passage into adulthood. That would be nice and clean, but it's not that simple. First, getting a degree obviously doesn't guarantee automatically getting a job. Second, job and even complete career changes are extremely common. This younger generation knows this, and we can see it in their ongoing hesitation to head in any one direction. Older generations seem to be content with college-age people having a lack of direction as long as they are still in school. But expectations seem to change once they graduate. At this point we think they should have decided on a career path and be on their way.

This is where our expectations need to be put into check.

According to the National Association of Colleges and Employers, only 25 percent of college graduates will have a job in place at the time of graduating with a bachelor's degree.[1] And many of these people find a job because they are flexible and looking outside of their field of study.

Either way this leaves 75 percent of college graduates without a job.

We can look at this and call them lazy or aimless for working part-time in a coffee shop or full-time as volunteers not even making minimum wage, but the economy has impacted this to a large degree. College graduates find themselves competing against laid-off workers and others with much more experience. These experienced workers most often also have a college education or are pursuing one. This changed landscape has created a whole new set of pressures for this generation and has in some ways erased yet another clear rite of passage. This is, at least in part, why many in their later twenties still haven't settled into a career path, why some are seemingly directionless, and why many don't seem to have initiative.

We may not like this reality, and we may still have high hopes for our own kids and the college-age people we work with to overcome the hardships in unique and creative ways. But we have to look beyond our expectations to the realities they face. No matter how you look at it, it's clear this adolescent space in between is a tough place to be. And that time in between is getting longer and longer.

SINGLE LIFE IS PROLONGED

The rising average age of marriage is another clear marker of delayed adulthood.[2] In 1950 the median age of marriage was twenty for women and twenty-two for men. In 1970 the United States average had risen to twenty-one for women and twenty-three for men. By 2007 it climbed to the ages of twenty-five for women and twenty-seven for men and according to United Nations worldwide research the average for first marriages in developed countries are 28 for women and 30 for men. [3]

But the increase of median ages of marriage doesn't seem to necessitate a complete change in values as much as it shows the changing of the *order* of values. For example, the Pew Research Center found that eighteen to twenty-nine-year-olds today value parenthood more than they do marriage.[4]

This is different than previous generations and may be due to the increase of childbirths happening out of wedlock, which this article says happened in 51 percent of all births among people in this age stage in 2008. It's not that these people don't value a healthy marriage, but in their stage of life today, parenthood often comes before marriage.

This steady increase in the median age of first-time marriages reveals a change in the road to adulthood, and there is a spectrum of opinions on this issue. The ultimate debate is over what has caused this change.

On one hand you have people suggesting this is simply due to a loss of values by this generation. Some suggest the rise of the median age of marriage is because of an increase of sexual behavior and promiscuity prior to marriage. The experience of sex in college is an increasing pressure, and spending at least some time living with a romantic partner that is not their spouse is almost expected.

Others suggest that many twentysomethings are simply afraid of getting married too soon because more than half experienced the divorce of their own parents. It's no wonder they are hesitant to walk down the road of marriage after living through the breakup of their own families.

Both of these issues certainly contribute to the increase in the average age of marriage, and researchers have tracked their influence. However, my experience has shown that higher education is an even stronger influence. It has caused a major cultural shift in regard to when people are even looking to get married in the first place. I would suggest that this is even at the root of statistics showing the increase in cohabitation and the priority shift from marriage to parenthood. More and more people are clearly waiting at least until they graduate with their undergraduate degree and settle into a "decent job" before taking the step of commitment in marriage. In 1950 people were thinking about marriage and family life by the late teens and settled into it by their early twenties.[5] Today marriage at such an early age has generally become unacceptable—both to parents and children.

Another interesting element to consider is the evolution of the role of women in our society. Since 1984 the number of females in graduate schools has exceeded the number of males. Between 1997 and 2007, the number of male full-time graduate students increased by only 32 percent, compared to 63 percent for females.[6] In 1950 women desperately avoided being classified as *single* for too long because it could make them undesirable.[7] Few attended college and vocational opportunities were limited. But the fight for equal rights in the 1960s as well as other egalitarian efforts drastically affected this. This has resulted in more women attending college than men.[8] Additionally the status of singleness and being career oriented is much more normal for women now and there is more vocational equality than ever before.

Sure, most college-age people think about and desire to be married at some point, but most are not seriously considering it until after they complete a degree. And as more and more people get married after completing college, the age most expect to get married rises even if they are not personally pursuing a degree. It seems that the ever-changing landscape of life created by higher education has prolonged crossing this sociological benchmark. Most college-age people view marriage as a time of stability which is desired, but from their perspective it's also a time where autonomy, spontaneity, exploration, and essentially all liberty ends. Interestingly, parental pressure to obtain a degree before marriage also greatly contributes to this thinking. Parents want their child to become his or her own person, get through school, figure out what they personally want, and then at some point get married. But not until after these things are finished and figured out.

We must understand the reality that these pressures often delay consistent adult living in this generation. The reality is marriage most often brings a sense of stability and consistency into our lives—especially for men. In the book of Genesis we are told that God created a woman because, "It is not good for the man to be alone" (Genesis 2:18). Well, today's alone period is longer than ever before. And at least one of the ways this shows up—often more obviously in guys than girls—is inconsistency. The natural accountability of the marriage partnership is delayed by the rising age of marriage.

So what should we do? Start a dating service? Reinstitute arranged marriages? Push people to get married earlier? No. It's simply that we have to recognize and accept the implications that higher education has on relationships, and the issues of inconsistency that singleness often brings.

INCONSISTENCY AND INSTABILITY IS THE NORM

Marriage, careers, and having children all bring consistency into our lives. Time and energy are generally spent differently in light of these life responsibilities. With higher education now pushing these later into the lives of this generation, inconsistency, or at least the perception of it, has come to mark the lives of eighteen- to twenty-five-year-olds. But as we seek to relate to young people, this is where our understanding of what has affected their thinking about consistent adultlike living becomes crucial. It's one thing to know that people in their twenties move around a lot, change jobs often, and are likely to move back in with their parents at some point during those transitions. But it's another thing to realize the deeper searching and loss of belonging in society that those inconsistencies reveal.

We can get frustrated at the instability of those in this life stage, but we must realize college-age people are looking at future responsibilities as just that—*future* responsibilities. Whether they are in school or not, college-age people clearly view this stage as time to enjoy things while they can—today. Tomorrow just has too many unanswered questions for them to sprint in that direction. I'm not suggesting this is ideal. I'm only stating the reality of the situation. We can sit back and criticize these people for "not growing up" and moving toward adulthood fast enough, but it's just not that simple anymore. There is a reason they're not in a hurry.

We actually do the same thing. Before we head in a new direction, we want to figure things out. Until we do we don't feel like it's wise to move in any direction. Their definition of *wise* may differ from ours. It could potentially be misguided, and if that's the case, there is a need for us to lovingly walk alongside them. But it's usually not that simple.

This stage of life is focused on self-exploration. It's an inconsistent, unstable, seemingly aimless, and possibly dangerous journey. But this is because there are a lot of unanswered questions needing to be sifted through before twentysomethings feel comfortable moving forward. And many find themselves not even getting past the first step: determining what they want. If they don't know what they want, they don't even know what steps to be looking for. We get a sense of what we want or need through experience and exposures. But limited experience in the workplace or exposure to pain can cause college-age people to hesitate, sometimes shut down, wander, or float through life until they can sift through all the unanswered questions.

When I find myself growing impatient with a college-age person who doesn't seem to be moving in any direction, I ask myself these questions:

- What if this person had no one investing in him growing up?

- What if she's never been taught the importance of working hard?

- What if his parents never emphasized the importance of initiative—even if they thought they did?

- What if her parents did all these things but with an overwhelming helicopter-like parenting style that causes younger people to disengage?

- What if his parents abandoned him for their own careers, so he simply doesn't see career as the best thing to pursue right now?

- What if she watched her parents go down a career path that provided for the family but didn't satisfy them emotionally?

- Or what if he was raised in a home where he didn't have to work for anything and was handed all his desires on a silver spoon?

These types of questions have led me to check myself before making presumptuous conclusions about any one person. They don't excuse irresponsible behavior, but they help me balance the expectations I put on someone. Sure this is generally an unstable and inconsistent time of life. We can't change some of the cultural influences that make it so. And we can't change the past experiences they have grown up with. But we can now walk alongside them with a desire to learn more about where they are, what pressures they feel, what they are desiring, and what has brought them to this point. Choose to come alongside them with patience and consistency, even when your desire to step back and hurl demeaning words their way seems justified. Your compassion and understanding is what allows the consistency of your life to be a bridge into the life of a college-age person.

PROLONGED FINANCIAL DEPENDENCE

We can obviously no longer characterize this age-stage of life as being self-sufficient like it may have been when you were this age. And this makes sense, or it should to some degree, after the previous sections. In the midst of extended educations with higher costs, exploring different career options, and moving around to find something or someplace that clicks, everyone still needs to pay the bills. This is why 73 percent of eighteen- to twenty-five-year-olds (both married and single) have had their parents recently help them with finances, but I find that even those who are not financially supported by their parents, think they should be (or wish they could be).[9]

The delaying of careers and extended educational needs has created a much longer dependence on parental financial assistance. One report done by the American Federation of Labor and Congress of Industrial Organizations (AFL-CIO), an organization working with 12.2 million union members, states that one in three workers under the age of thirty-five are living with at least one of their parents for extended amounts of time.[10] Granted, this would include high school kids working, but shows a prolonged dependence on parents for financial assistance.

This could be a result of a lack of baby-boomers retiring at the top of corporate chains. It could be a result of the hardship to find a decent paying job.

It could be revealing a lot of things, but one important issue is the amount of debt being accrued by people in their early twenties due to higher education.

Those who don't have parents who can afford to pay for their education are pursuing loans because they feel like they have no other choice. According to The Project on Student Debt, 67 percent of people graduate from college with debt. That debt averaged more than $23,000 for the class of 2008, a 24 percent increase since 2004.[11] This same research group has also found 37 percent of public and 55 percent of private school graduates start their careers with "unimaginable debt."[12] The unfortunate news is the costs for college are rapidly increasing. In fact, the cost for college is rising faster than the costs for medical care.

Some of the debt being accrued is simply out of laziness. I know plenty of students who just don't want to work so they get a loan and live comfortably for the time being. Or instead of doing the legwork and seeking financial aid they apply for another loan. It's easier to live shortsighted like this—for a while anyway. Applying for some type of grant or scholarship, instead of loans, can help but doesn't solve the problem. The maximum Pell Grant, which is the most common direct aid for low-income students, was $5,550 for the 2010–2011 school year. And while the maximum Pell grant did increase slightly every year between 2007 and 2011, it is far from keeping up with the quickly rising costs of higher education.[13]

According to the College Board Advocacy and Policy Center, the average yearly cost (tuition, fees, room and board rates) for full-time students in undergraduate public in-state schools was $16,140. And for those attending private four-year colleges it was a whopping $36,993.[14] Getting loans for this amount of money might not be quite so overwhelming for those seeking to be doctors or lawyers (although some recent grads in these fields might push back on that statement), but for most other professions this is an extreme burden to pay back. But students more than ever feel like they are left without an option. They feel like they have to continue getting more education in order to get a job . . . and will get a loan if necessary. This might make sense if it was truly an investment with a big payoff. But today it's tough to get into any career path without a degree, and we find college grads looking for those same jobs high school grads were working at the turn of the millennium.

All this to say, finances are a pressure and there is a practical need for extended assistance from parents. And perhaps the most important thing to keep in mind here is when someone is financially dependent on their parents, they are going to think about life much differently than if they were self-sufficient. Even dependence on student loans will impact a college student's thinking about pursuing financial independence and what we have traditionally called *adulthood*.

The space between what I have described in this chapter is probably quite different from what you remember the majority of your generation being like at the same age. You can probably think of a few of your friends who struggled through this space between, but it was not so widespread.

We all know that college-age people have many elements of maturity. If you spend time with a college-age person he or she will likely shock you with great wisdom and maturity in many different areas of life. But these areas often get overshadowed because of the lifestyle they are forced to live in a culture that has normalized the pursuit of higher education. Understanding that adding another necessary level of education has changed the way people think about adult life can help us see through circumstances to some of those areas of maturity. Nevertheless they are clearly in between a fully dependent childhood and independent adulthood.

CHAPTER 4
THE WHO OF THE TIMES

We've seen how higher education has extended the process of moving toward independent adulthood in a number of ways. Obtaining a college education has now become a necessity in our culture, leaving college-age people in a new and unique stage of life. Moving on from a high school identity and moving toward something in the future, college-age people find themselves seeking significance. This search for an identity looks vastly different from person to person, but one thing is common in all: It is ultimately about discovering who they are, what they value, and what is meaningful to them personally. Through exploration in a variety of areas they will eventually come to conclusions for themselves. In the meantime they cling to what they can. And each person clings to different things for meaning and significance.

I could write this entire book using statistics and explanations of what is happening in this new age stage of life, but the actual lives of real people bring even the best research numbers to life. I want to introduce you to five people who represent common characteristics found in college-age people. It might be easy to assume these five people are the way they are because of their pasts, personalities, or genders. However, this is not necessarily true. While some of their tendencies could be attributed to these factors, I've found these same characteristics and tendencies in college-age people of all types. I have chosen these individuals specifically because I believe they represent a variety of characteristics commonly found in college-age people today, regardless of background, personality, gender, or other commonalities.

These five profiles may not represent all college-age people. But as you meet them, you'll surely recognize the ways in which their mindsets about life have been impacted by the need for higher education, as we've discussed. Watch too for the general characteristics they exemplify. These are the characteristics we'll address in the remainder of the book.

STEVEN: "I'M JUST ENJOYING COLLEGE LIFE."

I first met Steven in a coffee shop near UCLA. I was sitting with an acquaintance of his when Steven walked in with his girlfriend. Arm around her, he confidently scanned the coffee shop for someone he might know. He was a husky guy, dressed in baggy jeans, worn-out skater shoes, backward hat, and a tight t-shirt with an unzipped hooded sweatshirt almost falling off his shoulders. He was comfortable in his own skin, and it showed. His girlfriend was obviously into him. He had one arm wrapped around her, and she was snuggled up under it with both her arms wrapped tightly around his waist. Our mutual friend saw him walk in and called him over to our table. Both Steven and his girlfriend were very nice and were comfortable meeting a new person (me). They ordered their coffee and ended up joining us at our table. Over the next two years I had the privilege of getting to know Steven better.

Steven was raised just outside St. Louis, Missouri. He came from a pretty conservative family that was financially comfortable. Steven's parents seemed to have the ability to pay for all his needs growing up, but also helped him develop a sense of responsibility for himself and made him work for what he got. His relationship with his parents also seemed to be good. His parents were still married, and he talked with his mom weekly and his dad about every other week or so. He also had a good relationship with his younger sister. He was protective of her and was a little nervous about her going off to college.

At twenty years old Steven was a sophomore in college, living in an on-campus apartment, enjoying campus life and all it brought his way. His life was centered in the Greek world of fraternities and sororities, parties, major sporting events, and general campus life. He did enough school work to get by, but was clear that his reasons for being in college were more for the experience of college life rather than an education or future vocation. He wasn't necessarily interested in subject matters discussed in class. He preferred enjoying life day to day, minute by minute. He didn't have any long-term goals for education. He did have a sense of personal responsibility, but didn't have the discipline to move in any particular direction. He was enjoying his freedom. He was more interested in social aspects of night life than the intellectual ideals presented in daily classes.

Steven talked about how amazing it was to meet people from everywhere. He had friends from different parts of the country and many from different countries and cultures. He was adamant about not letting class get in the way of his life. He despised the idea of working during these years because that would simply hinder his social life and the depth of experience it brought. He believed he had to capitalize on all these "once in a lifetime opportunities." For him, this meant enjoying his freedom as a college student. In fact, I clearly remember a statement Steven once made. He said, "You don't get a redo on the party you missed last weekend."

Steven did enough school work to please his parents and to pass classes, and his conversations with his parents centered around class and family matters. Of course they knew he had friends and did things with them, but their conversations steered away from the parties Steven attended or the late nights out with his girlfriend. He wasn't out of control with drinking or doing drugs, but he dabbled.

Steven's life probably wouldn't have been much different if he had attended a community college and lived at home. His priority was simply enjoying the freedoms this new stage of life provided.

As long as he met some minimum requirements in school he could do whatever he wanted. The most meaningful thing to him was his friendships and having fun. If those were taken from him he would have been devastated.

SHERIE: "I LOVE LEARNING. THIS STUFF TOTALLY MAKES SENSE."

Sherie was as petite as they come. She couldn't have been an inch taller than five feet. She had a sweet demeanor and was well respected by her peers. She had one of those personalities you couldn't help but enjoy being around.

Sherie grew up in southern California, just north of Los Angeles. Her parents divorced when she was eight years old. She remembered it vividly. She came home one day after school and realized her dad had moved out that day. It was abrupt and abrasive. She remembered her feelings, questions, and tears. She loved her dad very much and was deeply confused by the breakup. At the time she had no idea what had happened or what the issues were that tore her family apart. She remembered at eight crying herself to sleep for weeks afterward.

Her mom loved her and was very involved in her life. Sherie describes her as a great friend. Sherie also maintained her relationship with her dad. She visited him every other weekend and enjoyed those times. She referred to her dad as Poppa and had an endearing love for him. She was naturally gracious to all she encountered and her relationship with her parents was no different.

I came to know Sherie through the college ministry I used to lead. As an eighteen-year-old college freshman, she'd only had one boyfriend in her lifetime and was more interested in the educational side of the college experience. She had friends and went to different parties and gatherings with them. Sherie was the sober one, often driving her drunk friends home after the party. But these social activities weren't what really excited her. What really got Sherie excited was learning about the ideals her professors were presenting in class. She enjoyed thinking through the implications of academic topics. She poured most of her time into completing all the work required in classes and did so with excellence. She had good relationships with many of her professors because she was so engaged in the content they were presenting.

Sherie was intellectual and enjoyed learning. She tended to be a bit idealistic and seemed to be constantly conforming to what was being taught. She could critically think through the information being presented in class to a degree, but was also highly influenced by the thoughts of professors. She found it difficult to decipher the information she was hearing, which resulted in her often taking everything at face value and as truth. Some might call her naive. I would say she was easily influenced.

Sherie didn't know what she wanted to do as a vocation, but she wasn't concerned about it at this point either. The most meaningful thing for her was learning about concepts and ideas. Our conversations were largely based around her processes. I didn't say much, but instead listened to her ideas and thoughts about what she was learning. I wanted to be careful of continuing Sherie's tendency of accepting whatever someone in authority taught, so I tried asking questions that helped her think through things for herself. I asked questions such as, "Why do you think that?" Her thoughts were all theory, but lacked personal conviction. She was learning a lot, but was easily swayed. Her different learning experiences could be a great catalyst for her to discover who she was and what she believed—or they could be dangerous if she simply accepted everything she heard without thinking through what she thought for herself. And despite her love for learning, Sherie didn't have any better sense of how she wanted to apply her newfound knowledge vocationally than any of her college-age friends. She was simply enjoying the learning aspects of college life.

One note: I used Sherie as an example because she was the one who stood out in my mind. But I have known plenty of college-age guys with dominant personalities who share the same academic interest combined with the tendency to be swayed easily by professors. The sense of meaning and fulfillment found in academics and the educational aspects of this stage of life transcend personality.

JENNIFER: "I'M NOT SURE. I HAVE TO PROCESS THROUGH THAT MORE."

I first met Jennifer while eating dinner with her parents. I had developed a friendship with her father at various sporting event parties. I first met him at a Super Bowl party, and he and his wife invited my family over for dinner.

Jennifer came downstairs as we were eating, kissed her mom and dad goodbye, briefly introduced herself to us, and then left abruptly. Over a few years I got to know her pretty well. She was extremely sharp and had a great wit about her. She thought through things well and was definitely her own person.

She was raised in an upper-middle-class home. She describes it as consistent, and attributes this to her father's good career and her mother being a stay-at-home mom her entire life. Jennifer was the middle child between an older brother and a younger sister. The siblings had separate interests but got along well and enjoyed being together. Jennifer had a pretty strong personality but wasn't very outgoing. I guess you could say she had an inner strength, a critical one to be specific. This became more and more evident during our conversations as she went through college.

She was engaged in the ideals of her professors, but always approached class from a critical—some might say arrogant—mindset. She stayed an arm's length away from anyone else's opinion. There were clearly some professors she respected, but only those who had ideas that challenged her in new ways. She also respected those who taught classes with direct application to her life. She would disengage if she didn't find new challenge and practical application. Unlike Sherie, Jennifer would not conform to anyone else's theories for any reason. She didn't seek to please anyone and for the most part couldn't care less what a professor thought of her. She didn't even really care about the grade she received. She did well in the classes she was interested in and barely passed those she wasn't. Sitting back and comparing her own thoughts with the thoughts of others made her feel good and gave her a sense of fulfillment.

Jennifer tended to have issues with discipline and perseverance, especially in areas she didn't find interesting. Her life was totally centered on what she wanted and what she thought. She would have a great relationship with a person who had characteristics she personally valued. If she didn't respect another's ideas or values, she wouldn't have much if any connection with them. Jennifer tended to be idealistic in her thinking and internally critiqued anyone who thought differently. Having said that, at times I did see her think through something that was said and over time change her opinion. But it was always on her own timing.

Jennifer had some vocational ideas. She had a few different areas of interest, but nothing to provide a clear or practical direction. She was okay with that because she was confident in her ability to think and make choices and knew something would come in time.

JAMAAL: "I HAVE TO WORK FOR EVERYTHING I GET."

I have so much respect for Jamaal. He was raised in the projects just outside of Atlanta, Georgia. His father was put in prison when he was four, and his mother had and still struggles with a drug addiction. Jamaal was raised by his grandmother for the majority of his life. He stayed in school and was involved in a gang for a time in high school. But he eventually got out of that circle and kept out of trouble for the most part. He faced consequences for his decision to separate himself from the gang lifestyle—being mocked and beat up numerous times by his former gang family—but is thankful he got out.

I met Jamaal through an organization we were both speaking for. We met when he was twenty-three and attending San Jose State University. He clearly knew what he wanted to do with his life and had enrolled in school with a very practical mindset. He was seeking knowledge and skill sets that directly assisted him in getting where he wanted to be. Jamaal always wanted to earn a college degree because, in his mind, that was how he could make more money. He was fighting all sorts of odds with his background but was working hard for everything he had. Jamaal worked part-time to make it through school and pay for his studio apartment and other bills, so he had to take night classes. He didn't have much time, money, or desire for the social aspects of collegiate life. He had a very humble approach to learning, but was solid in his own thought processes. He took everything in and then sifted through it in light of who he was as an individual and what he wanted.

Jamaal was hopeful of a prosperous future. He found a great deal of meaning in working hard toward his goals. His identity was largely found in his perseverance, independence, and personal pursuits. I often wondered if Jamaal had a sense of who he was as an individual beyond the circumstances of his past. (Despite the opposite nature of their pasts, I had the same question about many students I met who had been handed every opportunity in life.) I wondered if his identity was more about his actions and reactions to life than about who he actually was as a human being. Jamaal was so focused on what he was *doing* that he didn't have much time for anything else in life, especially *becoming*. He was so busy moving forward that there was no time to process other important aspects of life. To spend time with him I had to pursue him and often had to adjust my schedule to fit his. I sat down with him often and frequently found myself wondering if things would work out for him the way he hoped.

KEVIN: "I'M NOT SURE WHAT NOW."

Kevin was good at sports and had been ever since he was young. He had been an all-star Little League baseball player and was also on numerous traveling soccer teams growing up. He traded soccer for basketball in junior high and continued playing baseball. He was a star athlete in both sports. But football was the sport of choice in Kevin's Alabama high school. A lot of his friends grew up playing, so when Kevin stepped onto the football field, many were far beyond him in skill level. That didn't last long. By his sophomore year in high school Kevin was once again superior to most of his teammates in yet another sport.

By his senior year Kevin had received offers from major universities for three different sports: baseball, basketball, and football. Tough decision. After a long and tedious process he finally accepted a full baseball scholarship to Arizona State University. Kevin's team was runner-up to the University of Southern California in the College World Series during his freshman year, 1998. He finished his college years at ASU and then moved to Southern California because of a job offer. I met him through a mutual friend, and we became friends.

I watched Kevin process through the realities of life after college. He had so many hopes during college. He had hopes of reaching the big leagues, and if that didn't happen, he had a college education to fall back on. He thought he would be fine, regardless of what happened. He could always get a job if baseball didn't work out.

Kevin had just begun a job with a marketing company when I met him. Within nine months he realized it was not what he wanted to do with his life. But he would have stayed with the company if they hadn't laid him off. It wasn't long before he found himself without a steady job, no identity in sports to fall back on, and searching. Like many college graduates his dreams and hopes of what a college education would provide him turned into feelings of depression and isolation. Everything Kevin depended on for his sense of identity, security, and meaning was now gone. And yet he had to move forward. He had to face the real world.

WHO DO YOU SEE?

Do you see someone you know in these profiles? Even if the specific circumstances of their lives are different, do you see the core struggle they face? The search for meaning in this age group is a struggle, and people deal with it differently. But they are all searching. Whether the focus is on the experiences of fun, academics, personal interests, or work, college-age people today are clinging to whatever they can hold on to. They need the love and guidance of older adults to help them look beyond their tendencies and develop into whole individuals. It's a lifelong process, but we can help by seeing the need at the core of whatever tendencies and struggles they show.

CHAPTER 5

MUDDIED WATERS– DETERMINING A LIFE DIRECTION

What are you going to do with your life? It's the dreaded question for any college-age person. And it's a huge tension point between generations. The older generations are asking, "Seriously, you don't know?" And the younger generations are asking, "Really, that's all you care about?" The misunderstanding continues to push our worlds apart. How can we reverse the trend and bring these generations closer together?

Hundreds of scenarios with college-age people come to mind, but a few examples stick out in my mind. John was facing a tremendous amount of pressure from his parents to figure out what he was going to do with his life as he finished his junior year in college. He was only somewhat excited about his major, and he was beginning to question whether or not he *really* wanted to head in that direction.

John's father was very successful in his career and was paying for John's education. He wanted the best for his son, and he obviously wanted his son to get the most out of his experience in college. He also clearly wanted his investment to be worthwhile. So John's father pushed him to determine what he was going to do with his education. He asked John frequently what direction he was heading in. Naturally, this pressure created big tension in their relationship.

Julie was dealing with a different pressure at the end of her collegiate senior year. Well, sort of. She was from a broken home, and her mother couldn't afford to pay for school. So Julie had no choice but to apply for numerous grants, loans, and financial assistance through different government programs. Her mom had a tough time supporting Julie and her two siblings as they grew up, so she was strongly encouraging Julie to head in a direction that made more money than she had made. Her mom didn't have a college education and was excited about all the possibilities this degree would provide for her daughter. So she pushed Julie to figure out what profitable thing she was going to do with this education she was working so hard to obtain. The reasoning is understandable looking on from the outside, but Julie's relationship with her mom was getting more and more strained.

We can look at the hearts of these two parents and clearly see where they were coming from. We understand that John's dad had personally experienced the benefits of a college education and wanted the best for his son. And what parent doesn't want her daughter to avoid the hardships she had to endure? Julie's mother understandably was excited about better possibilities for her daughter. The hearts of these parents weren't necessarily in the wrong place.

So what's the issue?

The problem is these parents didn't understand what they were *actually* asking their children. They were unintentionally asking their children to bypass and shortchange a long, complex, and necessary internal growth process. Both John and Julie understand that their parents find it meaningful for them to have an education, a good job, and to be able to support themselves and possibly a family someday. Most parents think this is the responsible, adultlike thing to do—a sign of maturity and growing up. But students see through a completely different lens. Their priority is not direction, but discovery. This fundamental difference causes confusion and friction in these relationships, and it's easy for parents to miss this important distinction.

GENERATIONAL DICHOTOMY

It's not that college-age people don't understand or even agree at some level with their parents on this issue. They desire direction in life and would love to be able to give an answer to what they're going to do with their lives. And they, of course, want to have their needs met. But first they must figure out what *they personally want.* Answering this question is by far the most meaningful thing in their lives. Asking them to come to a conclusion before they figure this out violates them to the core.

Discovering what they want is the hinge that will one day open the door to a life of meaning—or at least they hope. They are thinking, *How can I know what I'm going to do with my entire life if I don't even know what I want yet?* This question must be answered before they can confidently provide an answer to these pressuring questions about their life direction.

You can see the tension coming—you may even feel it rising as you read. This one gets at the core.

College-age people often look at parents or other older adults stuck in careers they don't love or find fulfilling. Twentysomethings see that their needs have been met, but they also see how much their mom or dad would prefer to be doing something else professionally. They see people stuck in careers or activities they don't enjoy, which is precisely what college-age people want to avoid— and will try to avoid at all costs. They would rather do something that satisfies them personally than get stuck in a career that only makes good money. Truth be told, they actually want both, which we will discuss later. But when given the options, they are more afraid of being unhappy than being unsuccessful. They don't want to dread going to work every day. They want to be excited about what they do. They want to be passionate about what they do and have an impact on the world through it.

This may be a bit idealistic, but who doesn't want this? Isn't this the very reason parents make sacrifices for their kids?

It's not that parents don't want these same things for their children, but they see things from a more practical standpoint. They are looking forward to future responsibilities their children may have. Parents have walked farther down the road of life with its demands, pains, and responsibilities. They see what is coming and hope their children will be prepared enough to avoid some of the pitfalls and hardships they faced. This perspective isn't bad, but it can put a lot of pressure on college-age people.

SEARCHING FOR MEANING

Meaning for parents often is rooted in the practicalities of responsibility. Meaning for college-age people usually is rooted in idealistic desire. Parents are thinking about responsibilities to others in the future and therefore want their child to choose a direction. The college-age person is in the process of discovering his own desires, accomplishing his personal goals (once they find or choose some), and discovering himself as an individual. Twentysomethings understand they are better off with an education, but they are hesitant about it if it marginalizes what they believe to be important about themselves. The same is true with a career path. The last thing they want to do is marginalize what they think is important about who they are and how they're uniquely wired. They don't want to simply get a job that pays the bills. They want to do something that's meaningful to them.

But they need to figure that part out.

Many of the college-age people I know view the pressure of parents to choose a direction as essentially asking them to bypass this process of discovering what they want and need. From their perspective the parent is asking them to negate their desires and possibly undermine who they are as a human being—for a job.

Think of it this way. Imagine you are looking to purchase a house. You do a little research, ask around, and get a realtor. You schedule an appointment to go see some houses. After your day of looking around you see some things you like and some things you don't. You are thankful for the realtor's time, but decide you need a little more time to figure out what you want in a home. In fact, after looking around, you're not sure if you even want to buy a house. The money could be spent on so many other important things.

But imagine the realtor hounding you to make a decision. Imagine him continually asking you, "Which house are you going to buy?" Imagine that every time you see this realtor around town he brings it up. What if you ran into him at your favorite restaurant and he said, "You should just move in a direction and pick a house. You'll never find a perfect one."

At best you would have a dreadful pit in your stomach every time you saw him because you would know where the conversation was headed. You may not avoid him entirely, but you'd certainly try to avoid talking to him about the subject of houses. At some point you'd probably even question his motives. Why? Well because you still had too many unanswered questions to make a choice. Not only did you still need to figure out what you actually wanted in a home, you needed to do some more research on financing, neighborhoods, school districts, and more.

If you can imagine what this would feel like, you can get a glimpse into the pressure and frustration college-age people feel when it comes to parental pressure to choose a life direction.

College-age people actually value much of the same things people of older generations do. But first things first. They must first discover who they are, determine what they want, and then they'll pick a direction. (We will discuss the different stages people go through to determine these things in the next chapter.) Some might suggest that this is different from purchasing a house, because there are responsibilities they need to take care of today. They would suggest heading in a direction—any direction—to pay their bills and then maybe find something more meaningful down the road.

This idea may be appropriate in some cases. But we must understand from a college-age person's perspective that it's just not that simple. Let me explain an important distinction college-age people make that previous generations didn't.

VOCATION VERSUS CAREER

Committing to a career path only for the sake of heading in a direction might appease outside pressures for a time, but college-age people fear that this will inevitably lead to even more frustration. They don't want to end up forty years old and still stuck in *that* direction. This would mean that their dreams of a meaningful life turned into a nightmare. This is a fear that drives them to wait.

So in an imaginative and idealistic way they continue looking past a career for a vocation. This is an extremely important distinction to understand.

Vocation is a term used in pretty much all secular circles today, but it originated in Christianity. The word comes from the Latin word *vocare*. It speaks of a calling by God to an individual. It stems from a theological idea that God has uniquely created people with gifts and talents oriented toward specific purposes. This is exactly what college-age people, Christian or not, are searching for. They are looking for *that* thing they are *supposed* to be doing in the world. They are looking for a vocation in this sense of the word.

For the most part older generations looked at getting a job quite differently. They looked at it in more of a practical way, as a means to obtaining necessary finances. They looked at the job search in the traditional sense of a career. Of course they preferred to do something they enjoyed, but there was a bigger concern for supporting themselves and their families. If a job did that, they were satisfied. They sucked it up, went to work, and dealt with it.

This is exactly what college-age people *don't* want to do.

Career is a term that refers to a person's course or progress in life and it is usually used in the context of remunerative work—meaning a profession you do for the purpose of gaining wages or a salary. Like *vocation* our English word for *career* also stems from Latin. The Latin word is *carrera,* which means race—as in "rat race." Most eighteen- to twenty-five-year-olds see too many people in older generations who seem to have their monetary needs met but have lost a sense of meaning and purpose in their lives. This is viewed as giving up a truly meaningful life for a career. And they don't want to get in that *rat race* of life. In fact, they want to avoid it at all costs.

Keep in mind that few college-age people will be able to define these differences in so many words. But they feel the emotion of it deeply as they search for what they are going to do with their lives. It might be a bit ideal for a person not to account for future responsibilities in the pursuit of *that thing* they're supposed to be doing. And it might be fairly ridiculous to dismiss all sense of today's responsibility in lieu of pursuing dreams. But figuring it out is all a process. The reality is college-age people, particularly in their late teens and earlier twenties, are looking for a vocation not a career. To them the pressure to choose a direction seems like a cop-out and a tragic undermining of who they are as human beings.

DIGGING DEEPER

This is an interesting and often complex dichotomy to walk through. Parents understand it to some degree but also think there has to be a balance. They want their children to do what makes them happy, but they also come at the questions from a different perspective. Supporting a family was an early reality for their generation—it was the reason for education, jobs, and careers. It was not only the right thing to do, it made sense, it was logical, and everyone was on a similar path—or at least expected to be. When a couple was able to provide for their family, it not only meant responsibility was taken care of, it also provided a sense of meaning and purpose in life.

Today this is different. College-age people see marriage and family as way off in the future. If they do decide to get married, they want it to be a partnership of sharing responsibilities and pursuing dreams together. It's still an idealistic possibility that requires them to discover their own identity first.

Many people in previous generations have gone through what's referred to as a midlife crisis. Today, the quarterlife crisis has taken over. And while older generations are driven crazy by the directionless searching and idealism of young people in the midst of this, they have experienced the same—just at a different stage of life. I have to look at this and wonder if fewer people in the younger generation will go through a midlife crisis because they are asking the hard questions earlier in life. The need for higher education may be delaying adulthood, but it is also providing the space and environment to grapple with these questions. It's what the new age stage is about.

Understanding this stage of life as a search for identity and meaning can allow us to step back, relax, and enjoy the discovery process a little. Sure, it would be great if suddenly our children woke up with all their questions about themselves answered. But this just isn't realistic; nor is it meaningful. In fact, it's not even what parents *actually* want for their children.

Keeping this search for self in perspective allows us to recognize that college-age people are in a critical time in life—one that takes a lot of time, and it should. They need to know more about who they are before they can figure out where they'll find meaning in their lives. Developmentally, this focus on who they are and what they want is normal; it can be healthy and even necessary. In the next chapter we'll walk through five stages of identity formulation that will help you understand this process. But before we do, let's look at what we can do to ease some of the tension.

Following are some questions I think people of older generations, especially parents, need to ask honestly before applying pressure on college-age people to determine a lifelong direction:

- What do I value about my child?

- Do I allow my child's life and results to reflect on me so much that they dictate my relationship with and my counsel to my child?

- Do I really value my child for who he or she is today, regardless of what he or she does or becomes?

- Do I place a higher value on what I personally want for my child than I do on what he or she wants?

These are hard introspective questions to ask, but they are necessary if we are going to have deep, long-term relationships with college-age people. Most parents and leaders want college-age people to be independent adults. But in order to get them there, we must allow and perhaps help them to go through that process.

LIFE TAKES CARE OF REALITY

I used to get worked up and frustrated by the seemingly aimless living of some college-age people. Out of frustration I would often give my opinion on what they should be doing. And, by the way, I would offer my advice whether anyone asked for it or not. I don't think I'm alone. We simply want to solve the problem at hand and give our perspective because we think it's what they *need* to do.

This can be like talking to a brick wall or worse.

Ever gotten a response like, "That's not what I'm looking for" or "You just don't understand" or maybe just a nod and silence that lets you know you missed the point? Out of a desire to help we bring practical solutions to their problems. We think we're helping, but our answers try to draw them out of their idealism. And this is not something they're willing to do yet. We don't get it because, well, they don't either. So more often than not we miss the point because they don't even know what the point is in the first place.

This is where parents often throw their hands up in the air. They are left wondering what their child needs from them. Nothing they do or say seems to help.

But after, oh, a few hundred conversations with college-age people I've finally begun to realize an important truth: Life has its way of naturally bringing people down to earth and it doesn't need my help. What I mean is that the experiences of life are the best teachers. The natural circumstances and consequences of life are one of God's ways of teaching us. It's why our parents can share all the wisdom they've gained, but it isn't until we get older that we realize our parents are smarter than we thought. It would be easier for us if we would actually listen to the advice of others before going through hardship, but most of us seem to prefer learning the hard way—through our own experiences. This is certainly true for most college-age people.

I have a formula that I think applies well to the college-age stage: Knowledge - Life Experience = Arrogance. The fact is college-age people know a lot in theory but have limited experience in life. This is their natural place in life, but it helps us to understand the realities it brings. Twentysomethings are thinking deeply about everything under the sun. They are questioning everything, processing through many perspectives, and eventually coming to conclusions of *how* they *think* things should be. This leads to idealistic thoughts and assumptions, which are often expressed in ways that come across arrogantly.

Remember that young couple who didn't have any kids but had all the answers to parenting? You may even remember being that couple. Being newly married I remember sitting in restaurants with my wife, Barbara, and critiquing parents. I would think things like, *If that were my kid, I would . . .*

I was a perfect parent until I became one. Once we had our first daughter, Karis, life abruptly lifted me out of my idealism and dropped me into reality. All of a sudden I realized it wasn't so simple. There was much more to parenting than those public moments.

The point here is, sure, college-age people are idealistic. They think theoretically and simply don't understand many of the everyday practicalities of life. They think about life, jobs, finances, and many other things the same way a childless young couple thinks about parenting. They have ideas about how things ought to go or how they want them to be. They end up critiquing everyone that doesn't match their ideals and even shut out the voices of those who challenge them. But eventually this usually gets balanced out in one way or another. You can talk at them until you are blue in the face, or relax knowing that life will take care of much of this. As they grow in experience and face the everyday pressures of the world, they will learn to balance their idealism with reality.

So the next time you catch yourself gearing up to hand out a full dose of reality, step back. College-age people need your counsel and wisdom, but it has to come in a nonthreatening way. When we approach them with the intent of trying to help them see what's coming and what they need to prepare for, we face relational separation. It's not that they don't hear what we're saying. They do. The issue is that they're not at the point of listening. Instead, ask questions. Let them answer. Listen. Patiently walk alongside them as they process. When you prove you are there to listen, you may find a willingness to listen growing on the other side as well.

Life has a way of bringing extreme idealism into reality by itself. We've all experienced the feeling of needing to find out something for ourselves. Because of this, at some point, we recognized our need to buckle down and do what needs to be done. For some it takes longer than others, but for the majority it inevitably comes. Think back on your life—you may have had to learn this the hard way too.

THE BALANCING ACT

Idealism has taken a beating in the last few pages. But there are aspects of the idealism of young people that we should not squelch.

Don't you wish you had done some things differently when you were young? Is there anything you wish you had tried but didn't simply because it wasn't practical? Where in your life do you find yourself thinking of what could have been? This is where I would encourage you to listen to college-age people. You might find yourself not only understanding them better, but maybe even getting motivated again yourself. They can use some of your practicalities from experience, but you can also use some of their idealism too!

Like all relationships, it's a balancing act. So here are four things to help you practically balance your relationships with college-age people:

1. Reflect

Take some time to look at your own life from the perspective of a college-age person. Think back. Ask the reflective questions—*Who am I? Who am I becoming? What do I love? How could that shape my future?* You may not feel like it's practical at this point in life to make a career out of what you love, but how can you make it a bigger part of your life? As you reflect, think about the idealism of college-age people. Isn't there a piece of that you can appreciate in them and desire for yourself?

2. Practice Humility

Try starting a conversation by asking a college-age person *her* thoughts about where *you* are in life. How's that for balance? Ask what she thinks about the life you live, the direction you took, and how she would do it differently. Starting here, from my experience, is far more effective than us only telling *our* thoughts about *their* lives. But beware: If you ask, be prepared for the answers. It might be challenging for you to avoid becoming defensive, but it could be an open door to an even deeper and more meaningful relationship if you can listen humbly.

3. Be a Learner

Balance begins in the ear—literally. The tiny organs of the inner ear provide balance for our entire bodies. And your listening ear can provide balance for your relationship with twentysomethings. It's easy to get frustrated that they're not hearing us, but are we listening to them? Find out what they're thinking. Ask how they're feeling. Ask about the pressures they feel and who they feel them from. Find out what they're discovering about themselves. Ask them what interests them and what they value. Find out what things they've tried or looked into. Find out what resonated with them and what didn't. And, as hard as this might be, listen without providing any answers, insights, or opinions. Help them process through their own thoughts and feelings by asking more questions and listening. They don't want you to simply provide practical answers to their idealistic questions. What they want is for someone to help them work through what they are processing. They are in a state of intellectual gymnastics and are trying to sift through all sorts of things. If they ask a direct question, I've found it appropriate to answer the direct question. But if they are just talking about what they're thinking about, they're not looking for us to answer. They are verbally processing with us because they view us as a safe person to do so with. This is a great sign and in many ways an open door. We can help by listening. We can help by asking questions that help them come to their own conclusions.

Please understand that I only offer this advice because I know a lot of college-age people wish this was a skill their parents and leaders had. This is a skill I had to learn the hard way. Maybe you do too. The book of James speaks of a wise person being slow to speak and quick to listen. I think he's on to something here.

4. Reject the Pressure

Have you ever thought that the pressure you put on others is a direct result of the pressure you feel? This was a common theme in my interviews with parents. They have to fight to minimize the opinions of outsiders, especially other parents. Most of the parents feel a tremendous amount of pressure in this area, and often pass that pressure on to their own kids. They often feel like the viewpoint of others, such as parents or their own peers, dictates how they parent and even how they felt about themselves as parents. The same could be said about church leaders and the college-age people they are responsible for.

One parent's perspective on this issue was perhaps the most insightful for me. She said, "I had to learn that my value as a human being is not predicated on whether or not my children do what I thought they should do. At some point I had to distinguish between the path I would take and the path they are going to take. It's their path, not mine. Mostly, I had to realize that my self-esteem couldn't be found in the amount of worldly direction or successes or failures of my children."

This mom said it well. I'll leave it at that.

CHAPTER 6

ENTITLEMENT, EGO, AND THE PURSUIT OF PLEASURE

I recently watched an interview of a professional athlete talking about his transition to another team. His statements were gracious toward the team and fans he was leaving in order to pursue a more optimistic future with another franchise. Initially I was impressed by his word choices. I perceived them to show true humility. That was until he made a statement that changed my perspective—radically. Toward the end of his interview he made the following statement: "I'm looking forward to taking my talents there and continuing to work on my greatness."

There's no way on earth he actually meant to say that, I thought. I was trying to give him the benefit of the doubt by assuming he didn't. But the remainder of the interview proved that statement to be exactly what he meant to say. *Humble* wasn't the first word that came to my mind when the interview ended. In fact, that couldn't have been further from what I was thinking.

This man definitely has abilities and skills that can help out his new team. He certainly has something to offer his new organization. But his statements arrogantly suggested this new organization ought to feel blessed and lucky to have *him* and his *talents.* They undoubtedly were excited and may have felt lucky, but the ego and inflated view of himself was a bit over the top for me. This transition and new relationship between this player and organization might work out great. But my hunch is that it's only going to work as long as this player gets exactly what he thinks he is entitled to. If not, I expect him to take *his talents* somewhere else that he feels will value him the way he feels entitled to.

Athletes, especially at the professional level, need confidence to be effective in what they do. They must feel comfortable in who they are, what they do, and what they bring to the table in and through their abilities. But there are times I think athletes take it a step too far. All this may be easy for me to say because I don't have the freakish genetics of a professional athlete. Far from it, actually. However, it does seem this particular athlete's confidence has risen to a level where it could hurt him in the long run.

Unfortunately I often see something similar in today's college-age people. The generalization doesn't apply to everyone, but I find that on the whole, college-age people have an overinflated view of themselves that lends itself to a sense of entitlement. Every generation of twentysomethings is seen by the previous generation to have some terminal issue. I know people in the Lost Generation who call Boomers the Me Generation. I know Boomers who look at the Generation Xers as aimless slackers. I know plenty of people in all previous generations who view this younger college-age generation of Millennials as arrogant and filled with a sense of entitlement to everything. It's never fun to be stuck in a box and labeled. But all of these generalizations have been made because they are true to some degree. In other words, this generation hasn't been dubbed the "Entitlement Generation" without reason.

It's not that every generation has only one issue and is immune to the others. The Entitlement Generation struggles with aimlessness too, and the Lost Generation probably had a pretty good sense of entitlement. But as a whole, each generation is known for something. Entitlement is a major theme for eighteen- to twenty-five-year-olds today.

There are plenty of people offering suggestions as to how it got to this point. Some blame marketers for targeting children with advertising and materialism. They feel this influence has shaped this generation more than any previous generations. This is viewed as such a serious problem that certain countries such as Sweden are taking action to ban all advertising directed at children.

It seems likely that marketing, at least in part, is not helping today's young people. But it's a never-ending circle. Marketers in turn look for trends in generations and use that to shape their marketing. They know younger people feel a sense of entitlement to anything, so they work their product into a category that their target market does not yet have, but should feel entitled to. It's savvy, pointed, and effective in selling products. And it ingrains a sense of entitlement deeper into their Western bones.

Some have suggested that entitlement is an issue with parenting. It's the coddling of Boomer parents that has created this self-focus and overall disrespect for authority. At the core of this claim, people say it's the permissive or "helicopter" parents who hover over their children, desiring to protect them from any harm and please their kids with whatever they want. These helicopter parents don't mean harm and often confess they just want their children to have everything they didn't as a child. They might also add they don't want to treat their children as they were treated when they were growing up. Sociologists who point to helicopter parents as a cause of this sense of entitlement also say that the parents' desire for their child to have a fun, carefree childhood actually denies kids valuable lessons that will allow them to survive in environments where they actually have to work.

Others have pointed to parents from a different angle. They suggested that the entitlement issues are due to parents abandoning their children for their own careers and exaggerated ideas of material *needs*. The issue raised here is that the parents have been so infused with materialism that they have abandoned their children to uphold a standard of living. Love for their children somehow translated into purchases. They point to the rapid growth of mothers working to pay for all the material desires of her family, and suggest this has created a generation that lacks little and therefore expects everything. These individuals might also point to the fact that many parents have left the rearing of their children to teachers, professors, and future employers.

Others don't point to parents as much as they do the times. They would say that there is a sense of entitlement because this generation of college-age people has been raised during one of the most affluent times in history. They've had instant gratification and know no different. They've been told by culture that if they want something bad enough they can get it. There is no doubt this is pointed directly to upper-middle and upper-class families and suggests that the blessings this generation has enjoyed has cultivated ungratefulness and expectations of nothing but the best.

Finally, there are those who view entitlement as a basic lack of biblical understanding of God's grace and human depravity. From a biblical perspective we understand we are not inherently driven to do good in God's eyes, but are instead sinful by nature. This is grossly contradicted by a culture that tells us that we are, in fact, inherently good. This bleeds into a misunderstanding of what we actually deserve as human beings. Those who point to this spiritual cause say this younger generation thinks just because they work hard or do something well they should have everything go their way and get what they want. They make God the employer who should give and provide all opportunities.

To point to any one of these things as *the* creator of this cultural epidemic would be fairly ridiculous. For each individual there are likely multiple reasons and degrees of circumstantial factors. But regardless of the exact causes, there is an undeniable sense of entitlement in this generation. They don't just want something; they feel they deserve it—now. Why should they have to wait for it? Their sense of entitlement, ego, and the pursuit of their own personal desires can be seen in the constant questioning of judgment by those in authority, complaining when things don't go their way, circumventing their immediate supervisors to seek what they want or think should be done, expressions of ungratefulness, and assertions that they should be treated as equals to those in authority.

I want to reiterate my early statement here that this cannot be applied across the board. There are plenty of college-age people who work hard, are humble in their relationships with those in authority, and are grateful for the things and opportunities they are given. But every generation has its thematic problems. And this generational sense of entitlement is something professors, parents, church leaders, and employers have to adjust to and learn to deal with.

ENTITLEMENT IN THE WORKFORCE

With the hopes of what a college education might bring, college students jump through the necessary hoops to obtain a degree. They may have no idea exactly what they want to do, but deep inside they believe this is the golden ticket to a prosperous and fulfilling future. Despite the workforce reality that a bachelor's degree doesn't guarantee anything, students (as well as many parents) still have a false sense of hope about what this degree will bring. This is one of the reasons people feel like it's well worth going into heaps of debt. A college education is viewed as an investment into a student's hopes for the future.

People are certainly better off with a bachelor's degree than without one, but if this path is not walked cautiously people can find themselves with debt their salary won't pay for. This is happening more and more. In fact CNBC recently aired a documentary called, *Price of Admission: America's College Debt Crisis,* which featured experts suggesting the amount of school debt might be more damaging to our economy than the recent housing market crash. People rack up the debt because they believe this is what provides the opportunity to get a job that will easily pay off the debt. Unfortunately more and more people are discovering the brutal reality that the payoff isn't as automatic as they thought.

Most people deeply believe a college degree will get them what they want in life. Everything seems possible, and their hopes are high to land their dream job. In the minds of most college-age people, that job not only pays well, but provides the platform for influence as well as freedom and schedule flexibility. Sounds like a dream, right? Not to them. It's an expectation.

In fact, although it might not be verbally articulated in a job interview, this is often assumed and even expected to some degree. College-age people often portray a *professional athlete syndrome* in job interviews. They feel like their talents and abilities ought to be valued by the organization. They paid the price of time, did the hard work making it through college, so a company should be honored to have them as employees.

This tendency surfaces in the reality that very few college-age people are willing to pay the price of time to climb the ladder of an organizational chart. Some are repulsed by the idea of the corporate world. At a deeper level, however, college-age people don't feel like they should start at the bottom. If they are forced to, they tend to be discontent with the hours, limitations to their freedom, salary, and amount of input in decision making that they are allowed by their employers. Inherently many think they have a lot to offer, and if their expectations are not met, discontentment can easily lead them to looking for other companies that would properly value their talents and skill sets. Growing up having an online voice into any subject they want to address, they now assume they'll have a voice in the workplace too. Great frustration can occur if they are not given the ability to share their opinions.

This is a major generational shift. A generation or two ago people were honored to have a company offer them a job. Today it seems as though people are thinking the company should be honored they would submit an application. People used to graciously accept a job because the company provided a job where their needs could be met. People were happy to start off in an entry-level position and were excited about any opportunity to prove themselves over time. Today the idea of proving yourself through experience doesn't exist. Actually, it's quite the opposite. Most twentysomethings think they should have more responsibility than given and potentially a higher influence into the overall direction of the company. Because they've thought through some things in theory, they assume they know best—and others should recognize what they have to offer. They might not say it in so many words like our athlete friend, but they feel it inside.

Again, these tendencies do not apply to every person in this generation. I can list plenty of people who absolutely do not fit these descriptions. But as much as I'd like to say they're the majority, I don't believe they are. As much of an advocate as I can be for college-age people, this is an issue that is difficult to deal with and address with them. It's a deep issue, rooted in the core of this generation's mindset. On the surface they can be humble and meek when starting a position. But after giving it time, if they are not being used the way they feel appropriate, the deeper sense of entitlement seeps out. I've seen it in the workplace, in interns, in counseling sessions, and with those I've mentored over the years. Unfortunately, it's not hard to see.

And it's even easier to see when I know full well it exists within me. Recognizing some of the same tendencies within myself has led me to have more grace with others.

We can and should ask twentysomethings questions about why they feel entitled to something. We can certainly try to help them understand the importance and value of consistently proving themselves and working their way up over time. We can let them know that along that road we tend to learn valuable lessons that are needed to sustain our effectiveness. We can affirm and praise them when warranted, and give them an appropriate place and method for sharing opinions. And we can definitely confront the issue with a gentle firmness. But the bottom line is that an internal gratefulness cannot be instilled by anyone but God. Some inherently have this sense of gratitude for any opportunity, but we simply cannot infuse this into someone who does not have it. It has to come from within.

UNDERSTANDING THE INTERNAL CONTEXT

There is a constant battle inside every college-age person. If you could look inside their hearts and minds you'd see little soldiers duking it out on the internal battlefield of self. On one side in dusty brown are the old guys—the people they used to be. On the other side in camouflage green are the new guys—the people they are discovering and becoming. And mixed in to confuse the troops in a whole variety of colors are the other "selfs." These represent the people others see and expect them to be, as well as what they themselves wish they could be. The battle is an ongoing process. Sometimes the old self has the upper hand; sometimes the new self is gaining strength. But most college-age people don't want others to see that internal conflict. Like most of us, they want to look like they have it all figured out even when they don't.

College-age people will at some point find themselves in a place where they have intensely thought through who they are and who they are not. A place where they feel like they have a decent grasp on their strengths and weaknesses, likes and dislikes. There comes a point when they become comfortable in their own skin (or at least their perception of it), value who they've become, and want to be in a place where their strengths can be used. But there is still a lot going on inside.

Typically in the first few years after high school there is more conscious self-discovery than perhaps all the other years of life combined. This encompasses both strengths and weaknesses. The weaknesses stand out and often cause an outpouring of depression and isolated feelings. It's similar to when you receive five compliments on the shirt you're wearing and then one criticism. The one bad comment tends to overshadow the good ones. This same thing happens internally when college-age people discover their own insufficiencies. It doesn't feel good. In fact they will avoid having to deal with them at all costs.

This is important to understand because members of this generation will have a strong desire to be used in their strengths but won't want to grow in their weaknesses. This often causes them to concentrate on their strengths, sometimes even in an inflated manner. And if they don't find themselves in a place where their talents and gifts are used as they see fit, they feel underused, undervalued, misunderstood, and stifled. But since we don't have x-ray vision to see what's going on inside, it can be difficult to understand.

When a teenager thinks his parents are stupid you can tell right away. His eyes roll, his disposition spews out arrogance or frustration, and he might even come right out and say it. College-age people, for the most part, are different. They can be vocally upset about ways in which they feel undervalued or treated unfairly, but their communication is usually more controlled. They begin to tell their friends and other peers or coworkers about their frustrations. This, of course, breeds dissension and bitterness, but it's the way most of them vent their feelings. (This is also a human tendency that you probably deal with too!) They can also be passive-aggressive when communicating their frustrations. For instance, they might vocalize their complaints in anonymous online surveys put out by their employer, in emails, on a personal blog, or even through a Twitter update.

This can make it tough to know what is really going on inside a college-age person. This again is where listening is key. Ask questions; get to the bottom of the tension. Listening will help you have a glimpse into the true internal struggle and the places you can best offer encouragement and affirmation.

A MEETING PLACE

I've had dozens of interns over the years and have worked with thousands of college-age people across the country. Working with and mentoring young leaders can present unique challenges. It's tempting as a leader, employer, or even parent to push young people into leadership because of their gifts and talents. But in doing so we often fail to work on their character. This only heightens the issues related to a sense of entitlement. Even a very talented twentysomething has areas of character that need work. (Don't we all?) But the feeling that their ideas and opinions should be heard without question is only heightened by being put in a position of leadership. It brings up tough confrontations that need to be approached with love and brutal honesty.

That may sound harsh. But I've learned that while this generation doesn't like to be confronted about their weaknesses, they do like to hear it as it is. They may still need to process what you've told them which may include talking to friends or putting thoughts into cyberspace. They do this because it's their way of working through things. They are used to speaking their mind on digital platforms. I'm not suggesting it's always entirely appropriate, but Facebook, blogs, and other social media outlets are this generation's way of passing on information as well as processing it for themselves.

We can still help them see the value of face-to-face private confrontations. The best way to do this is by modeling it for them. We can share times when we've done it with others, times when we've appreciated someone doing it to us, and we can do it directly with them. Either way we can model what healthy, private, loving confrontation and conflict resolution looks like. It may be one of the most important life skills we can teach.

Entitlement in this generation does have a positive side as well. The idea that as individuals we should set our priorities and expect them to be respected by others can be a positive thing. We can learn a lot about relating to this generation from companies and organizations that are finding good ways to balance and even capitalize on aspects of this sense of entitlement. Many companies are adapting their processes to meet the lifestyle requests and expectations of this generation including flexible work schedules, telecommuting, and paid volunteer time. That is good news for

health, communities, and family life. These companies are seeing that they ultimately get more out of their younger employees
when they adapt. We would do well to recognize the areas where
we can adapt and compromise and, in doing so, improve our relationships with the younger generation.

Another area companies are meeting Millennials is in providing platforms and environments where opinions and voices of all
employees are listened to and validated. Positions still matter, but
all people have a right to speak and be heard. Businesses have discovered that this younger generation cares less about money than
previous ones and simply wants to be a meaningful part of something bigger than themselves. They want to have influence and feel
like they are valued. And for them, being valued is shown in more
than a salary. Salary is obviously still a piece of the puzzle, but there
is more to it and companies are beginning to appreciate what this
generation brings to the table.

I've seen these things in my years of experience leading in
churches as well. The value of giving college-age people and other
younger people a voice—and actually listening to them—can't be
underestimated. One of my favorite ways to do this is to gather
five to ten twentysomethings at my house for dinner and ask their
thoughts on everything from a message I taught to the overall
direction and philosophy of our ministry. I've come to understand
the importance they place on people listening to them. And, I must
say, I'm often blown away by their wisdom and insight. So much so
that I've come to realize that I need them in my life! Some of what
they say is obviously drenched in idealism, but more often their
insights provide much needed clarity and direction for me. Plus, a
good dose of young idealism can never hurt an "old" guy like me.

ALL IN THE FAMILY

Parents I've talked with who have been effective in adapting their
relationships with their college-age kids point to an important

transition. They have intentionally made the effort to go from being a parent to being more of a companion. They realize that their child still needs and desires them to be around, but in the role of a friend and confidant instead of a manager and provider. One parent said, "My kids value me as their mom, but don't want me to counsel as a mom. I've also realized that I have to stop providing as a mom too." I asked her to clarify what she meant by "provide as a mom." She replied, "I can't just give them everything anymore. If I do I just enable them to feel entitled to everything and that means they won't ever feel like they have to work for things." I find this theme is common in parents who continue to have a great relationship with their kids, regardless of faith background.

Setting up boundaries in areas such as finances also helps set boundaries in other areas as well. This healthy separation does at times create tension. One couple said their son seems to pout when they won't give him rent money. But at the same time, this couple said that their son has articulated how much he appreciates the way they parent. Of course our kids are going to keep taking money and expecting it from us as long as we are freely handing over the cash! But by creating a healthy boundary, we take a huge step in breaking the cycle of dependence and opening the door for healthy boundaries and relational freedom in other areas as well.

For some of the parents I interviewed, that freedom includes seeking the counsel of their kids. They will ask questions about how they ought to parent their younger siblings, seek their advice on faith issues, pursue their opinion on vacation spots, and even ask them their opinions of how they are doing as a husband or wife. It's not that these parents stop offering their advice entirely. But they've put a priority on listening and opened the door to a new form of give and take. And this, for many, has been a very effective way of meeting their kids in their entitlement. In fact, every parent I've talked to who has adapted this concept into their relationship says that their children actually listen to them more now.

Fascinating.

Part of feeling entitled to certain things usually means you stop listening to people when they challenge you or give you advice you don't want to hear. However it seems that if they are given a voice, college-age people's ears tend to open as well. It takes humility on both sides.

And according to one mom, it also takes a little bit of humor too. "I think as parents we just need to have a sense of humor about the entitlement issue," she says. "At this point in life our kids will only listen to us so much and at some level we have to realize that they'll learn some things. My generation has some issues too. I've learned to laugh at those. So, I know we have to work on this issue with our kids, but at some point we just have to let it go, loosen up a little, and just laugh."

CHAPTER 7

THE ARDUOUS PROCESS OF PURSUING SELF

Identity is not an issue during the college-age stage of life; it's *the* issue. Much is processed throughout these years, but there are four underlying questions at the center of every search:

1. Who am I?

2. What do I value?

3. How am I unique?

4. How do I fit into society?

Answering these questions leads a person to self-awareness, a solid grasp on who they are, as well as a direction in life. Identity is critical to everything. All of our decisions and goals are driven by who or what we identify ourselves with. Whatever gives us our sense of identity will also determine what our life will look like.

In other words, it's *really* important to think through.

I recently had lunch with a guy in his first semester at school. Three months of being away from home had him realizing some things about his life. First, he was beginning to see how good he had it at home. His room at home was much bigger than the dorm room he was now sharing with someone else. His mom cleaned the bathroom he used at home. A stark contrast to the bathroom he shares with three other guys and which nobody cleans. He talked about how much he had taken for granted the meals his mom and dad cooked. He talked about how he used to balk at his mom when she would tell him he had to come home for dinner. Now, because he's been away for a while, he wishes he could have dinner with his parents every night. Cafeteria food three meals a day just doesn't come close. There were all sorts of things like this he was thinking through after being away from home. Things weren't nearly as bad as he used to think they were.

Time and space can cause realities like these to hit all of us at different points in life, but during the college-age years there is a massive influx of reality. They might seem obvious and simple. However, they are the beginning of something deep and complex. A person learns more and more about himself through these kinds of reflections. He learns what he values and what he doesn't.

As I sat and ate with this young man I enjoyed hearing his new realizations about life and what he was discovering about himself. Smirking inside, I listened as he verbally vomited his thoughts out. It's not that I was smirking *at* him, I just know that this is only the beginning. This stage of life will bring more thoughts that will cause his previous ones to change. He was certain about some things at that moment—things that would certainly be different soon. That was only the start of the beginning. There will be hardships and heartbreaks, laughter and joy, and a whole slew of circumstances and experiences that will help him learn about who he is, how he's unique, and what he values. All of it will ultimately guide him in his life direction.

College is a time of mind-opening opportunities that lead to the mindset of a lifetime. What a fun stage of life! One that is filled with potential and ripe for shaping. And if I continue to listen to him and his thoughts, the reality is I will also be shaped. There are some brilliant thoughts to come out of his mind!

College-age people have a sense of identity anchored in their family to some degree, but they have been inching away from family since junior high. Now after high school, it's a full pursuit of who they are apart from their family. This search leaves them in between two worlds, especially with the blurred lines of dependence as we saw in chapter three. Having left their identity of the past and struggling to find footing in an identity today, they find themselves clinging to what they hope will come. That is, if they can figure out what they'd like that to be.

This space between identities holds huge potential. People in this place can head in any direction. It's an exhilarating time of pursuit, exposure, and discovery. So why is it so scary? Well, people can lose who they *actually* are in this pursuit of trying to find themselves.

At first glance that may sound a little confusing, so let me explain.

BREAKING DOWN THE SEARCH FOR SELF

Forming an identity can be simple and clean for some, but for others it's filled with speed bumps constructed with mass confusion. All kinds of theories explain identity formation. The best-known come from a psychologist named Erik Erikson who laid out eight distinct stages of development, starting with infancy and moving on through childhood, adolescence, and adulthood. Erikson's stages describe how identity is developed over a lifetime.

Another scholar, James Marcia, took Erikson's stages and broke them down into four specific states of identity development. According to Marcia, the typical adolescent shifts in and out of these four states of identity formation:[1]

1. *Identity diffusion.* In this state, a person has no real sense of who he is as an individual, nor does he have a desire to figure it out. He struggles with commitment and isn't searching for a sense of self.

2. *Identity foreclosure.* Many high school students are in this state. They have an identity, but it's based solely on the expectations and values of others—parents, friends, high school

culture—rather than on their own exploration or values. In this state there is also no intentional searching for who they are as individuals apart from others.

3. *Identity moratorium.* In this state a person is exploring her options but has yet to come to conclusions about who she is and what she wants in life. It's a state with lots of searching but little, if any, commitment.

4. *Identity achievement.* In this state, the person finds a sense of identity in society. Her identity will still develop, but the basic understanding of who she is and how she fits into society is in place. She demonstrates high commitment and is no longer intensely searching.

I have found these descriptions to be helpful in understanding the process of how someone forms an identity. It has really helped me as I have sat down with thousands of college-age people, talking about their lives. My desire is never to categorize people, but rather to use these stages to better understand where they are in their search for identity. These four stages have served as a catalyst for me. I am certainly no scholarly expert, but I have spent the past twelve years learning about the college-age stage of life through sitting down with its members to listen and hearing them out.

While Marcia's four stages have been helpful for me, my extended time with college-age people has brought me to form a list of the stages I see them passing through. I now want to walk you through five different stages of identity formation for college-age people. I don't differentiate these stages (or people) by personality types, but instead by their mindsets in regard to who they think they are and what they identify themselves in or with. I've found people generally progress through these stages, but some may be in multiple stages at any given time. Others can find themselves in a new stage each day, depending on what day or hour you talk to them. Regardless, I think you will find them helpful in recognizing where the college-age people you love so much are in their search for identity. I call these five stages the Substitute, the Floater, the Explorer, the Tentmaker, and the Theologian.

The Substitute: Becoming What Others Demand

Like a teenager shifting back and forth between his party persona and his church persona, the Substitute has yet to commit to a solid sense of identity. This person has been said to have a "patchwork self."[2] The Substitute's identity is like a patch that is sewn on, and different patches are worn depending on where the person is at any given time. This person has *substituted* the search for who they *really* are with what someone or something else has asked them to be. This makes the Substitute extremely susceptible to peer pressure and inconsistent behavior. While this stage of identity formation is typical for a mid-adolescent (generally fourteen to seventeen years old), it often continues well into the late-adolescent stage (eighteen to twenty-five years old).

The Substitute often makes decisions in order to fit into a social atmosphere and does so without truly understanding the implications of those decisions. A social atmosphere could be school, church, fraternity house, a sporting venue, home, a particular friend's house, or just about any place someone is in the company of other people. Each social atmosphere has its rules and expectations for behavior, and the Substitute is particularly attuned to these rules and expectations. Because Substitutes have a sense of identity in the atmosphere they are currently in, or feel the most pressure from, they forgo a search for who they are and simply adapt to wherever they are. This person substitutes *who* they are for *where* they are.

For instance, a party requires certain characteristics and behaviors in order for a person to truly fit in and play an active role in what is going on. The requirements of the party are different from the requirements of, say, a youth group meeting or a gathering of friends in your own home. Because Substitutes want to fit in and function in all social atmospheres, they adjust their identity to fit the environment. They act and react in specific ways that fit the atmosphere of the moment to make sure they are respected in that atmosphere. The bottom line is true identity is substituted for what the atmosphere respects or requires. It's a chameleon-like stage of identity where change is the norm. The Substitute can appear one way around parents, another around one circle of friends, and yet another around different circles.

We can see the Substitute in action in college students who join fraternities or sororities in an effort to find an identity on campus. They can easily substitute their individual identity for that of the group. They may bounce from meeting the expectations of parents, to peers or boyfriends or girlfriends. The social atmosphere requires a high sense of commitment, and the Substitute explores his personal identity little outside of that context. Again, the danger is that Substitutes substitute who they *actually* are for whatever the social atmosphere demands that they be. And once a Substitute leaves that atmosphere, he has no real sense of who he is as an individual.

Some would suggest this can just be a people-pleasing person with a passive personality. That may be true to some degree, but it's deeper. The Substitute hasn't consciously sought out who he or she is as an individual. That's much deeper than a people-pleaser who knows who she *actually* is, but then struggles with violating her identity for what others desire or demand. The Substitute doesn't have a sense of self.

If you, as a parent, have a child who fits some of these characteristics, you may want to take a careful look at the ways you pursue parenting. Being overbearing or controlling is a common tendency in parents that can contribute to the Substitute's lack of identity. Maybe you've been a bit of a helicopter parent, constantly placing a high demand on your child to do and be certain things and constantly hovering over to make sure your standards are upheld.

The danger of this parenting style is that it never allows children to figure out who they are and their own uniquenesses. Instead they are given a set of standards they must fit into and live by. And the pattern with the Substitute usually continues beyond their parents, with the Substitute constantly exchanging who they are for the demands of others such as friends, teachers, and even church leaders. This certainly isn't always the case, but I have seen this pattern often. Because of this, once the college-age person realizes her parents are stifling the search for who she is as an individual, there is usually a relational fallout or separation at some level. I'd love for you to avoid that.

I'm not an expert at parenting college-age people, but as an outside friend who has spent countless hours with the Substitutes of today, here are a few thoughts for you to consider. If you do fall into this category of parenting, you might consider backing off in a few ways. Consider asking more questions about what your child wants rather than making sure he knows your opinion or desires. Chances are your kids already know what you're going to say anyway. Take into consideration that you may be parenting out of a fear of life's possible dangers rather than its possibilities, which is how your child likely views it. There is a place for both perspectives, but if you try to force your perspective to overshadow theirs you will inevitably face relational tension.

You might consider being careful of parenting out of a what-if fear of the future. Our natural desire to protect our children is a God-designed element of parenting, which can be great. But it can also be a sinful tendency that is driven by anxiety or fear or even a personality that needs to feel in control of everything, including our children's desires. Take some time to look closely at your motivations and tendencies to see how they might encourage or discourage the identity formation of your child at this stage of his or her life.

The Floater: Waiting to See What Happens

The Floater is the seemingly aimless person who just doesn't have a sense of direction. The Floater doesn't seem to be pursuing one either. This person is indecisive in just about everything. He doesn't have a grasp on who he is and therefore isn't heading in any direction. He is not interested in substituting his identity in a social atmosphere, although he can. He is not really pursuing anything at all.

The Floater tends to roam from part-time job to part-time job, take classes and then drop them, get involved in one thing and then quickly change course. Floaters are floating through life. The Floater is usually the one who stands out to people of older generations and is often unfairly the token poster child for today's younger generation. But it's important to know that Floaters aren't necessarily lazy or unfocused. This is clearly an indecisive stage of identity formation, but nevertheless it's a normal developmental stage.

A pattern with college-age people in this stage is they feel, for whatever reason, an immense amount of pressure to do something with their lives. Their response to this overwhelming pressure is often to put off making decisions as long as possible—procrastination showing itself in a total lack of commitment or exploration. They are asking some questions, but typically give up because there are just too many to answer. So the Floater lives day to day and puts little thought into what might come next in life. You may observe hints that the search for a more solid sense of identity is still going on, but identity is primarily found in their current circumstances. And the Floater is content with that.

The danger of this stage is that identity formation can't happen without identity exploration. Exploration takes intentionality and thought. It's a real effort to try on an identity and see how it fits. But the Floater isn't really looking for a fit—she's contently floating through life. The pressures are just too intense, and most Floaters don't find themselves in a place where they *have to* move in any direction.

If you know a Floater and want to help her move past this stage, you might consider a few things. First, make sure you love that person for who she is, not for what you hope she will be. This is critical. Floaters must know that you love them regardless of what they may accomplish or become. Second, find a time to sit down and ask questions. These have to be questions that are *not* loaded or agenda driven. To clarify, they can't be asked in a way that seeks to steer the person you are talking with in the direction you desire her to go. Instead, they have to be honest questions that stem from your desire to truly get to know what the Floater thinks and wants. To word this another way, ask questions, don't question her.

By doing these two things you will probably find your Floater opens up much more to you about what she desires in life. And, believe it or not, you will be a source of encouragement. Floaters long for encouragement, and that alone can move someone from Floater into the next phase of finding themselves.

The Explorer: Trying on Different Hats

This stage is the opposite of the Substitute. The Substitute commits to something without consciously exploring. The Explorer explores without committing. In my experience, those who find themselves in this stage are out of the teen years and in the earlier twenties. The Explorer can formulate his view of himself through school, but does so primarily through exploring different relationships and work.[3] Unlike the Floater, the Explorer is beginning to put more thought and intentionality into various parts of life. The Explorer is dating with an eye toward marriage and trying jobs that have some connection to his life dreams and goals. This level doesn't involve a fully realized identity, but it's a significant step toward developing one.

The Explorer stage happens when a college-age person goes through a process called differentiation and integration.[4] This is an abstract process that requires a great deal of cognitive ability.

Differentiation and integration begins as late adolescents start to place importance on the individual characteristics of people and social atmospheres around them. Rather than making emotional and impulsive decisions—like the Substitute and the Floater—the Explorer engages in a conscious thought process that takes place over a period of time. He starts to consider how he fits in with people and atmospheres—and whether or not he personally *wants* to fit in. Explorers look at everything from the values and attitudes they see in others to the duties required for a job. Then they begin to differentiate and integrate. They differentiate the characteristics they see from those they believe they possess themselves. After differentiating themselves from what is seen, they pick and choose which characteristics they want to integrate into their identity and which ones they want to drop. Explorers assess all of this information as either respectable and desired or unsuitable and undesirable.

Obviously, this stage demands a new level of self-awareness as well as some initiative. And that self-awareness is self-perpetuating throughout this stage. The more the person differentiates and integrates, the more self-aware he becomes. People of older generations often see this stage as erratic, showing a lack of commitment. Parents may find that it's flat-out scary. It might even come across as aimless and inconsistent.

All these reactions are understandable, but this stage shouldn't frustrate us. This stage is essential to healthy identity formation. It shows initiative, and it's a big part of the process necessary for someone to become his or her own person. The amount of time this exploration takes may not fit our personal timeline, but that's not necessarily important. The important aspect here is the development of discovering oneself. Explorers, by delving into experiences, relationships, and learning, gain a sense of who they are, what they want, and how they fit in the world. I'd also suggest the earlier a person goes through this process, regardless of how long it takes, the more time they will have to live a consistent life in a meaningful direction. It may even be that the quarterlife crisis period, when approached patiently and intentionally, will prevent a midlife crisis that could potentially have far greater consequences.

If the people you know and love are exploring all sorts of things and you find yourself impatiently waiting for them to land, I'd recommend readjusting. Try to let go and enjoy the process. You want your children to become independent adults. You'd probably say you "just want them to be happy." The Explorer stage, as scary as it might be, is a necessary stage in reaching these results.

So how do you adjust and allow Explorers to explore? My advice may sound vaguely familiar. First, consider letting go of your frustration over their lack of commitment and try to focus on enjoying the fact that they are discovering a lot about themselves. Second, ask them questions about what they are finding out. Ask them what they like, what aspects of their job or relationship they like most, or people they can't seem to get along with and why that's the case. You'll pay the price of time—possibly quite a bit of time. But in and through this relationship you can be that loving mentor voice they long for and need. And once an Explorer's differentiation and integration processes impact enough of their identity, they will begin to move toward finding a place of commitment.

The Tentmaker: Finding a Place in Society

This stage marks a balance between exploration and commitment. This person has gone through significant life experiences, which gives her the ability to make concrete decisions about what she wants to do when coupled with her increasing self-awareness. The Tentmaker tends to make choices she thinks click with her as an individual. She has gone through the process of differentiation and integration. Because a conscious thought process preceded commitment, the Tentmaker is much more likely to withstand pressures from others and remain committed to who she believes she is. At times this means standing by a new identity even when a parent disagrees.

There is another side to this though. Marcia suggests that this stage represents the end of identity formation. He refers to this as identity achievement. However, I don't believe this marks the final stage for the college-age person. Marcia bases his sense of identity achievement on sociological placement. He suggests that identity is settled when a person chooses a career, a relationship, and a living situation.

Now this is the point of identity formation we find ourselves in most of the time. It's at least the phase most people desire to be in and often push college-age people toward. It's where we want our kids to be and can get frustrated when they're not.

But besides these markers of identity, I would suggest there is a deeper longing necessary for true identity formation. Although finding a place in society points to a sense of stability and may even provide a temporary sense of relief and contentment, college-age people aren't settled with these benchmarks alone. Plus, who they think they are may not be who they *actually* are. They might dive into a situation they think clicks with them, but then find that it doesn't as much as they originally thought. The circumstances might turn out to be quite different than they hoped.

This stage then is a tent, not a permanent home built on a solid foundation. In fact this stage can be dangerous when a person is tempted to settle here. When the storms of life hit causing circumstances to change from what was originally perceived, the Tentmaker can easily go into a whirlwind of identity crisis. Feelings of achievement and contentment can quickly become feelings of detachment and depression. The result of changed circumstances becomes an endless cycle of crisis and shifting of identity (see Figure 7.1, page 103).

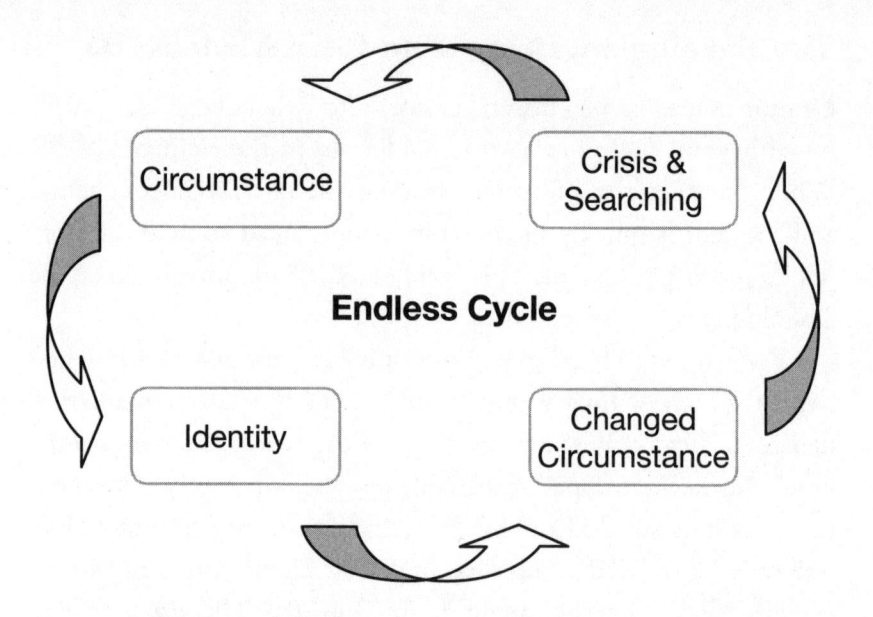

Figure 7.1. The Endless Cycle of Identity Formation

Asking people in this stage a few simple questions about identity can play a huge role in moving them beyond an identity in their current circumstances. Ask, "Who are you?" Clarify this by saying that you're asking who they are as human beings, beyond anything they do. Tell them to take away their jobs, their socioeconomic status, and current relationships, and ask them who they are beyond those things. Of course, these all play a role in who they see themselves being, but if they are not very careful this simply becomes a more culturally acceptable Substitute stage.

This is why I have added another level of identity formation, one in which a person's identity moves beyond sociological markers or individual circumstances. This next stage of identity is difficult to fully embrace, but I'd also suggest that this next stage is where college-age people, regardless of religious affiliation, are seeking to be—even if they're not able to verbalize it.

The Theologian: Being Who I Am Made to Be

Our job as leaders, parents, and pastors is to help college-age people move beyond the temporary tent-identity of their circumstances. When the storms of life come crashing, the circumstances change, and the tent is quickly blown over, people need something more stable, more permanent. This solid stage of identity is what the Theologian stage is all about.

When I say Theologian, I'm not talking about a person who's been through seminary and is up on all the latest theological debates. I mean it in the truest sense of the word: one who studies God. Our deepest hope for the college-age people we work with is that they'll know God and live lives that honor him. And that hope will only be realized when they find their identity in God alone.

By grounding her identity in God, the Theologian views what she's learned about herself in the other stages through an understanding of who God has made her to be. Her identity is in God, not in sociological pursuits. Her relationships, job, and circumstances still matter. But instead of letting people and atmospheres define her, the Theologian wants her faith to define these relationships and experiences. (For more on the pursuit of spiritual truth see chapter eight).

The Theologian will process her social identity through the lens of her spiritual identity. So as she moves toward a true identity, she isn't just hoping to fit in or find her place in society. She has a missional mindset, one that inspires her to seek out roles in which she can live out her spiritual identity as a child of God (see Figure 7.2, page 105).

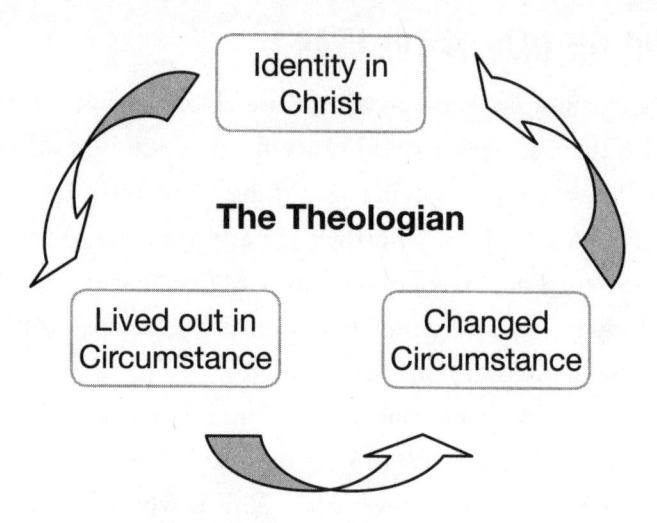

Figure 7.2. The Theologian

The Theologian can endure trials and changes in circumstances because circumstances don't define her. She finds meaning in something that doesn't change, no matter the circumstances. The Bible is packed with the idea that our identity as Christians is completely beyond the circumstances of this world. I understand that is much easier said than embraced. However, it is still the truth. In fact, we ought to pursue it ourselves. And we ought to allow college-age people to go through the hard and arduous task of figuring this part out.

To put this as practically as I can then, we ought to be careful pushing people to find an identity in society. Instead, I suggest we should do quite the opposite. I'm not suggesting we never help them find a place in society, but I am suggesting we not put the cart before the horse. Once they figure this spiritual aspect of themselves out, we can then help them find a place in society where they can authentically live out who they have been uniquely made to be.

This process is very long. It requires much patience. We have to pay the price of time. But it's necessary and worth it.

HITTING THE NAIL ON THE HEAD

Whether or not college-age people are able to think through life biblically, they do seek to find out who they are beyond circumstances. They are still seeking *that* thing they are *supposed* to be doing. They are seeking who they are, and they desire to live that out in society. They may ebb and flow between stages or progress through them in classic order, but college-age people clearly don't want to be defined or confined by them.

Let's go back to the conversation I mentioned at the beginning of this chapter. As I sat with this young man, I found I was listening to the very beginning of this process. This is why I smirked inside. There were many more conversations to come. I had to be patient. I had to listen before I spoke. I had to hear what he was really saying, what he was discovering, and what he thought it all meant for his life. I had to ask questions to help him process through it all. But most of all, I had to pay the price of time. It would be years before he landed. And in the grand scheme of things that's okay. The last thing he needed to do was substitute who he is with how his circumstances made him feel on any particular day.

My questions for him over the coming months and years included:

- Who do you think God has made you to be? I referred him to passages such as 1 Peter 2:4-11 and Ephesians 1:3-14.

- What do you want to place your hope in? I referred to passages such as 1 Peter 1:13.

- What commitments do you want to shape your life?

- What do you feel like others want from you?

- What do you feel like others want *for* you?

I asked him these questions because I've found one thing to be true: If we don't have a sense of how God views us, we will never have a proper view of ourselves. Additionally, if we don't have a biblical sense of who we are, we will lose our actual identity in the world. As a Christian, that's not something worth losing.

PARENT PONDERINGS

Patience is an important theme that comes up in this discussion. The parents I talk to confirm it, and I have personally had to concentrate on it as I work with college-age people. The need for patience is one that never goes away for parents. Patience fuels perspective. The bottom line among parents I interviewed was they had to intentionally step back and allow their children to figure things out on their own as they pass through these identity stages. Unfortunately most of them didn't learn this lesson until after years of frustration from trying to force their kids in a direction they weren't ready to go.

Another common issue is fear. Parents who hold strong religious convictions often experience a deep fear that their children will end up believing something different. This fear was particularly highlighted when I brought up the idea of the influence of their children's peers who come from different backgrounds. It can feel like a constant threat to parents. One father of a college sophomore summarized the conclusion well when he said, "I've really had to battle this because it's very scary when our kids start to question and doubt everything we believe. But I had to realize that I want my child to have her own convictions. She can't take mine. I want her to own her faith, and I've realized that her being exposed to other things forces her to process through everything for herself. She still asks me questions, but I try not to answer blatantly anymore. Instead I just ask her more questions about what she thinks. I can't allow her to live on my convictions forever."

Now that's some true wisdom from a parent who isn't letting fear stand in the way of bringing his and his daughter's worlds together.

CHAPTER 8

DISCOVERING PERSONAL CONVICTIONS

College-age people, regardless of religious—or nonreligious—upbringing, begin to explore all sorts of new questions. What do I believe about God and why? Do I *really* believe it, or just say I do because my parents do? What do I believe about myself and why? Do I even know who I am?

Most of these questions are up in the air for college-age people. They are greatly engaged with issues of values and beliefs, but few can concisely tell you what they personally believe and why. For those who can, the answers often change quickly and drastically. Thinking through all this can be a lengthy process for some. It can be scary and frustrating for parents and leaders. But it's important for us to understand that this is a vital part of the development that occurs during this age stage.

The ages of eighteen to twenty-five have become a time of mind-opening opportunities which can lead to thought processes with long-term impacts. It's a time when most people question and often struggle with their beliefs. They find themselves caught between the influence of their parents and a need to find their own anchors in life. This in-between stage of life offers a freedom to begin a search for who they are and what they believe—apart from everything they grew up assuming to be true. It's not that everything from the past is thrown away. But they need the freedom to put it all out there for consideration. Some of what they grew up believing gets shelved and left there until they figure things out for themselves.

The world appears black and white as we grow up. There is good and bad, nice and naughty. We think that way because our brains can only process information in a linear fashion: A+B=C. Because our young brains are limited to this linear way of thinking, parents and leaders teach and counsel us in this manner.

Growing up I learned an important aspect of life while eating: You never put your elbows on the table. This was, for whatever reason, wrong. My mom never explained why it was wrong. It just was. And it certainly was not something that was to be questioned. It was an appropriate parenting tactic when I was young. But as I got older, that tactic didn't cut it anymore. I wanted some answers. I wondered why it was wrong. I understood the conclusion, but I didn't understand the reasons.

In the late adolescent years, the brain is better able to process information in nonlinear, abstract ways. It begins to wonder *why*, and it recognizes that sometimes A+B=A. We realize things are not always as straightforward as we once believed, and the maturing brain begins to *expect* ambiguity as well.

In other words, college-age people are not only able to handle abstract concepts, but they're also no longer satisfied with simplified conclusions. They want to know the reasoning behind those conclusions. They are not going to accept a simple surface, black-and-white answer to a question they now realize has a lot of ambiguity. That's good news because it means they're ready and excited to dig into their beliefs in ways they never could before. And it's a process that's necessary for them to embrace their own convictions. It can also be dangerous because minds filled with far more questions than answers can get stuck in a whirlwind of confusion.

Look at it this way. College-age people who were raised with one perspective on questions of identity and meaning and life and God eventually become aware that this perspective isn't the only way of thinking. The answers to all of these issues might not have been as simple as adults made them seem. They begin to look at other ways of thinking outside the context in which they grew up. The exposure to new processes of thoughts, different opinions, and points of view is not only intriguing, but it's also exciting. The black and white world they grew up in is suddenly full of color. And they won't go backward. They have to move forward and explore the gray areas that life in full color creates.

This is where parents and leaders often come head to head with college-age people—or probably more frequently lose intimate connection with them. College-age people are in an intense search in their gray world, and if an older adult tries to give simplified answers to their complex thought processes, there will inevitably be a disconnect. Parents are often asked questions by their children to which they respond with a problem-solving, bottomline answer. Those answers used to work, so parents are often surprised when their child responds with a heart-wrenching, "Never mind, that's not what I'm looking for" type of answer. This can be disheartening. The parent simply wanted to provide helpful and practical advice. But this type of black-and-white counsel is no longer an effective influencer. It tends to rob thought rather than provoke it.

We are dealing with an age stage of life that provokes questions and reevaluation in some of the most important questions in all of life: *Who are we? What is our purpose? Why are we here? Where did we come from? Where will everything end up? What does it all mean for me today?*

There are four main influencers that will shape the thinking of eighteen- to twenty-five-year-olds as they seek to answer these questions:

1. Religious convictions

2. Philosophical thought

3. The sciences

4. Relationships

Let's look at the first three influencers first, then talk about how the fourth, relationships, can impact each of them. Then we'll dive further into the larger issue of relationships in the next chapter.

RELIGIOUS CONVICTIONS

Stephanie grew up in an Orthodox Jewish home. She loved her culture and held firmly to her religious convictions. These convictions had been a central part of her family for generations. She was not ashamed of her beliefs in any way—in fact, she was quite proud of her heritage. When she headed for college, she moved into an on-campus dorm and had a roommate she adored. They clicked immediately. They were both nervous about who they would have to live with, but both found themselves extremely relieved. By the second semester of their freshman year, they had become best of friends.

They had a lot in common, but their religious convictions were not one of them. Her roommate was Muslim and, like Stephanie, was rooted firmly in her religious beliefs. Both girls came to school with the hope of influencing peers to move toward their own religious convictions. They had countless late-night talks with topics ranging from socks they prefer to the roots of their belief systems. More and more, their religious beliefs became central to most of their discussions. Neither girl previously had experienced much, if any, exposure to the convictions of people outside her own faith traditions. But they found themselves more and more intrigued with what the other believed and why. Each girl held firm to her own beliefs but admitted to being confused. This exposure to a different belief system at such an intimate level caused them to think in new ways.

Stephanie made the following statement to me while talking in a coffee shop over a winter break: "After getting to know my roommate, I've realized how committed she is to her beliefs—in some ways more than I have ever been to mine. She's a really good person too. I never understood a lot of the background and the history of her religion, but getting to know her I'm realizing there is much more to her beliefs than I ever realized. It has really made me think about what I believe and why."

Stephanie told me she grew up being taught about her religion and a little bit about other religions. But she realized that what she learned about other religions was minimal and from an obviously biased perspective. In other words, her roommate wasn't as strange or dumb or naive as others made it seem to her as she was growing up.

Stephanie told me she wondered what her faith would be like if she was raised in a family with non-Jewish convictions. She was fairly confident she would have accepted those beliefs instead. She found herself questioning what she actually believed for herself. She was concerned that she believed what she does simply because it's all she ever knew. She never really explored any other religions because she grew up assuming they were all wrong. But she'd never really thought about it for herself and had never known someone who was so firmly grounded in another religion either.

Stephanie echoed much of what I've seen in college-age people, regardless of religious background. As a Christian I have seen this scenario countless times with kids who have grown up in the church. There comes a point where the apologetics class they took which gave shallow and biased perspectives about other religions just doesn't cut it anymore. Even those who previously delved deeper into the beliefs of other religions can have their world rocked when it becomes personal. Once they get to know people who follow another religion, everything seems to change. It's one thing to hear or read about how other religions compare with ours in a class. Knowing someone of another religion personally take things to a whole new level. When it comes to forming a worldview, no component is more important than the experience of religious convictions held by others.

What a person believes about God ultimately drives the way they view the world. Often for the first time in their lives, college-age people are exposed to other faith systems in an intriguing way. It is intriguing because as they learn about another religion in the context of a relationship, they discover that the faith of others is more rational than they anticipated. This relational connection makes other religious convictions so real—and confusing.

Some aren't swayed from their previous convictions at all. Some have their boat rocked, but stay strong. Others get swept out to sea.

Some people are so intrigued that they won't stop with just one exposure, but actually desire to know more about other beliefs as well. I've seen this search conclude in a number of different ways. Some are challenged and strengthened in their faith. Some completely walk away from their family's convictions, accepting those of a friend. Some give up entirely and try to separate from all organized religious beliefs.

I've befriended many people who fall under one of these categories. For those who turn their back on the faith of their childhood, I've found they were never as settled in their faith as others may have previously assumed. They may have been involved in church activities during high school, but most admit they did it mostly for social reasons or to appease parents. These individuals typically had a hard time grasping a personal faith during those years. They didn't want to hurt or offend their parents, so they respected their beliefs. With new freedoms, they are able to process what it is they believe for themselves.

I've met with countless parents who see this happening in their kids and feel as though their child's faith was stripped away. I know this isn't exactly comforting, but I suggest that sometimes faith was assumed based on certain actions such as church attendance or baptism. The new experiences and exposures of the college years reveal that faith may have lacked authenticity and depth.

On the other hand there are many who had an authentic faith of their own, but are drastically confused by these new exposures. This confusion can be short-lived or be long and frustrating for all involved. But in the end many become stronger in their convictions by walking through and facing the questions and confusion. The exposure to other faiths can help them become firmly settled on their own.

From a Christian perspective, we trust truth. We believe that it has nothing to hide. As leaders we can pray and walk alongside these young people in the midst of their confusion and questioning. We can avoid indoctrinating when college-age people ask us questions, and we can ask them more questions and seek to guide people toward the Scriptures themselves. That's a big difference, but it's easy to confuse.

College-age people often claim to be "spiritual," but usually not in a biblical sense. For instance, they view personal faith as more important than being a part of a faith community. Some even suggest that being a part of a faith community is hindering them in their faith development. While many college-age people do attend organized religious gatherings on a fairly regular basis, most seem to believe that no one religion holds the entire truth. Many accept a kind of universalism in which each religion has pieces of the truth, but none in its entirety. Of course not everyone is willing to say this outright. But from my experience, I would say the majority of the college-age population thinks this way. Other research also finds them to rely on their inner thoughts, feelings, and desires to sort out what's important to them and to be more content in their lives. UCLA has done some research on spirituality in higher education and compiled it in *A National Study of College Students' Search for Meaning and Purpose.* In this report they articulate this finding:

"Providing students with more opportunities to connect with their 'inner selves' facilitates growth in their academic and leadership skills, contributes to their intellectual self-confidence and psychological well-being, and enhances their satisfaction with college."[1]

Because they're engaging with their own feelings and thoughts and involved in spiritual issues and conversations, they believe they're being spiritual. But it doesn't mean they are rooted in a particular religion's articulated convictions.

The aspects that college-age people commonly find interesting about religions might surprise some. For the most part, learning about all the conclusions of a particular religion is just a starting point. For instance, they want to know what, if anything, a certain faith system thinks about Jesus or what happens after a person dies. Yet it seems this is just the beginning of the search. Many find it even more interesting to discover the history and traditions of these other faith systems. I've found this to be especially true with those who have grown up in a Protestant Christian home, which historically is not known for teaching about its traditions and historical roots. This is why we have seen a movement of college-age people who have grown up in a Protestant Christian home interested in faiths that do well at explaining their histories and traditions, such as Roman Catholicism or Orthodox churches. College-age people are also very interested in how a religion relates to and impacts the world around them. The relationship between social justice and religious belief is a growing area of interest to this age group.

Ultimately all of this is a search for a spiritual identity independent from their parents'. The religious beliefs they grew up with play a role in shaping their thinking, of course. But during these years, regardless of upbringing, they need to figure things out for themselves and explore thoughts outside of their upbringing, usually in the context of a relationship.

PHILOSOPHICAL THOUGHT

Another powerful influencer on worldview development is philosophical discussion. College-age people are typically drawn to philosophical topics due to their expanding reasoning capabilities and desire to think through abstract issues at a much deeper level. Granted, some are less stimulated by intellectual conversation than others. But for the most part college-age people are interested in talking about abstract issues such as ethics and morality. And, like exposure to other religious convictions, intellectual and philosophical thought can either affirm or oppose a young person's presuppositions about the world.

These influential conversations often first happen in a college classroom. Those who sit under a good philosophical teacher are often shocked at how deeply a person can think through a particular subject, how every question seems to be answered with another question. They hear ideas they've never heard before, discover perspectives on life, God, humanity, morality, and meaning they've never considered. They feel their minds expanding and getting confused—and it's thrilling! They listen to and engage in conversations about topics they've never explored. This is attractive to their minds at this stage. It's a catalyst into their own thinking and beliefs apart from anything they grew up with. Ultimately it plays a part in college-age people feeling like they are becoming their own individuals. And they are doing just that.

Even high school graduates who don't go to college will find themselves in relationships with coworkers, customers, landlords, roommates, and friends who will challenge their assumptions about ethical and moral issues. While college classrooms are natural settings, they certainly aren't the only place these conversations take place. They come with the age-stage territory. In my experience, the young people who weather this enormous mental expansion best are those with the foundation of *personal* faith to take in what they hear, look at it through the lens of what they believe, and come out with a far more thought-out faith than the one with which they began. These people will ebb and flow in their convictions, and usually go through times of mental confusion, and even frequent compromise. Philosophical questioning almost always leads to these things at some level, but the personal foundation of faith can be upheld and even strengthened.

On the other hand, those who only went through the motions as they were growing up tend to land differently. I find that if a personal faith was not authentically embraced prior to college, the process of navigating challenging philosophical thought is much more complex.

As parents we should be aware of how our parenting style impacts the way our kids learn about and live out their worldview as well as their faith. But while we have a faith responsibility *to* our kids, no parent can be responsible *for* their child's faith. We have to do our best to avoid the most common pitfalls: authoritarian parenting that drives faith based on shame or guilt or simplified answers that never get beyond the elbows-on-the table approach. As our kids grow older, we would do well to remember that they are not ours, but God's. We can influence their faith journey, but we cannot control it. There can be pain in that reality, but also amazing freedom.

Those young people who weather the storm of philosophical exploration and intellectual gymnastics also have something else instilled in them: They don't view philosophical thought as an enemy to faith. Instead, engaging in difficult conversations is viewed as a catalyst to faith and growth. Some can become arrogantly consumed in their own intellect and move away from previous convictions (see Colossians 2:8). There is a fine line between philosophical thought and absolute truth. When understood as an intellectual way humans try to make sense of the world, philosophical thought can work together with faith. If, however, human thoughts and opinions are taken as absolute truth and not viewed through the lens of faith, they can be confusing.

Jeanine was wrestling with a "zillion questions." She said so when she emailed me and asked if we could meet to talk through what she was learning. I agreed and about a week later she came to my office. She explained how she had grown up in a Christian family and had never doubted anything she grew up learning. Now at age twenty-two she seemed to be doubting everything. As I asked her questions about what was causing this, it became evident it was the thoughts of friends and professors.

She had relationships with people from all over the country and from all sorts of different backgrounds. She sat and listened to philosophy professors who were turning her thinking about God, eternal life, Jesus, and the Bible completely upside down. She ate lunch, hung out, and lived with friends who had come to completely different conclusions about all these topics as well. And Jeanine attended a Christian university. That is important to note because the upheaval of previous knowledge is not just found at secular universities or with friends from other religious backgrounds. It's an age-stage issue, regardless of where a person attends school.

Jeanine was blown away by the ways people had thought through things she'd never even considered. In her case, even though she was attending a Christian university that aligned with her parents' convictions, she was still exposed to thoughts she'd never explored. And many of them, for whatever reason, were different from what she had believed or thought up to this point. She realized there were other ideas about the origins of the Bible. She was surprised to find out there were differing views on the creation account in Genesis. She was totally shocked to learn that many ancient manuscripts don't include passages she has in her English Bible. She found herself questioning everything. She was interested in getting as many people's thoughts on these topics as possible.

The philosophical thoughts of people other than parents are a huge influencer in the lives of college-age people. The more exposure twentysomethings gain to other viewpoints, the more they want to know what other people think and why they think it. They quickly realize that not only their faith, but their entire view of the world was in black and white. And they are highly intrigued by the graying brought on by the plethora of thoughts on any given subject.

THE SCIENCES

Along with faith and philosophy, the sciences are an area where college-age people often face new challenges. Whether it's through atheists, secular humanists, agnostics, bosses, roommates, professors, or girlfriends' siblings, new relationships bring up new questions. And these questions often have some kind of foot in the science world.

I don't mean that they're necessarily scientific questions, but questions about life and faith and God and meaning can rise from conversations about anything from creation to human nature to political science. Those conversations often cause college-age people to see inconsistencies in the belief system with which they grew up. They sometimes point out faulty assumptions they've held for years. All that rethinking can again strengthen their faith, or drastically shake the foundations of a college-age person's worldview—or both. No matter how a college-age person handles the inevitable shake-up, they will need to make it through some hard questions aroused by science.

As leaders and parents we can set a foundation for college-age people by helping them view faith and science as aspects of life that can compliment each other rather than as opposing forces. Those who survive this particular storm of questioning are typically those who understand that faith and science aren't as black-and-white as they're often made out to be.

Everyone knows that science isn't flawless. Certain scientific theories that were once held as indisputable fact have now been proven false. Most scientists acknowledge that much of what they believe is their best guess based on their observations, and that it very well could change if the evidence changes. The "facts" of science are still just human observations, no matter how you look at it—educated ones, but observations none the less.

From a Christian perspective I have seen many students dump all their religious convictions because of conversations revolving around science. Too often this is rooted in an intellectual hypocrisy that is common in Christian circles. Christians often rail against science when it seems to contradict what they believe, but then embrace science when it seemingly supports what they believe. This creates an internal complexity within college students. They have seen church leaders and parents bash science at times and then use it to support their beliefs. This ultimately confuses them.

College-age people need to have the skills and confidence to navigate the sometimes-contentious world of science. In order for this to happen we have to help them understand that science is neither the devil nor an angel. It's human observation, and sometimes humans do, in fact, discover the truth about God's creation. Science never *determines* truth, but it does sometimes *find* it. This is an important distinction to make. It's a matter of worldview. And simplifying it like this for people, even briefly, can make a world of difference.

Perhaps most important to faith, we want people to view science beyond the evidence. I believed in the authority of the Bible long before I knew how to prove it because faith, not scientific research, defines my belief in truth. My faith is an internal conviction that goes deeper than other people's observations about creation. While faith and science can and should work together, they are based on two different perspectives of how a person determines truth. One relies on internal conviction and transformation to understand truth, the other on external data to prove it. It's futile to try to force them both to do the same thing when they are starting from completely different premises. This can be confusing for people but can make for a much richer and deeper belief in God.

Regardless of religious background or conviction, the sciences will play a role in shaping the personal convictions of college-age people. Those who keep their faith from capsizing in conversations based around science are those who keep in mind that all evidence is seen through a worldview—one that either assumes God is who he says he is, or one that doesn't.

RELATIONSHIPS

This process of discovering personal convictions is perhaps the most emotional aspect of parenting or leading a college-age person. I find that whether parents are fundamental conservative Christians, universalists, or atheists, they share a common trait—they have raised their children to value and embrace the beliefs they hold. But the way parents handle their child's questioning varies greatly. From a Christian perspective I have seen some parents handle this well, maintaining a great relationship with their children during this time of searching. I have also seen some who have literally destroyed their relationship with their children over changing and differing personal convictions.

I know one couple who has done some things exceptionally well and continues to have a great relationship with their kids. They are extremely solid in their faith, and the husband is an elder in a Christian church. When I wrote this book, their children were college age and just beyond. One was sort of floundering through what he actually believed. Another in college was reevaluating everything she grew up learning. But both of them had regular conversations with their parents about faith. In my interview for this book I asked, "What do you do when your kids have questions about faith or even land somewhere other than where you do?" Immediately the mom said, "The first thing we've learned is to not freak out." She went on to explain, as her husband nodded his head, how the kids disengaged and stopped talking about that issue when she did freak out. And when that happened, the parents were left in a position without insight into what was *actually* happening in the minds of their kids. Their parental opinion was shut out. I have seen this exact scenario happen far more than I'd like to admit.

"So what have you done that keeps the conversation going?" I asked. They have found the following helpful in continuing conversations about personal convictions with their kids during this time of searching. (Church leaders you should also pay close attention to these things as you lead college-age people in your context.):

- Make sure kids know that their relationship isn't based or affirmed on what they say they believe. This has allowed their children the freedom to be honest, which parents appreciate.

- Seek to have discussions rather than teacher-pupil or parent-to-child conversations. They assume the posture of a friend and in doing so engage with questions rather than providing answers or practical advice.

- Ask why questions such as, "Why are you asking?" or "What are you processing through that brings this up?" Open questions provide an atmosphere where kids can call and have a discussion that will help them think through things themselves.

- Realize you cannot make children believe anything, so don't try. Instead, these parents have sought to help their children think through things themselves. When they provided answers, they tried to express them as their own personal convictions. This let the children know what they thought, but gave the children freedom to come to their own conclusions and share them with their parents. The children understood that just because their parents aren't condemning unbiblical thoughts doesn't mean they are condoning them.

This kind of questioning and dialogue keeps the relational door open and allows room for growth.

CHAPTER 9

THE EVOLUTION AND ROLE OF RELATIONSHIPS

Let's say you're waiting for a friend at a local restaurant. You're quietly sitting in a chair outside, thumbing through your phone. Your friend walks up. You embrace and make your way inside. It's been a while since you've connected. You're excited to catch up. While you're standing in line to place an order, you begin the conversation by simply asking, "So how are things going?"

Not an abnormal question, right? A typical response might be, "We're doing well. Not a ton new, but everyone is doing great. Kids are healthy, doing well in school. Work is . . . "You can fill in the rest.

But what if your friend, with eyes wide open and a huge smile, looked at you and said, "Wow. Things are amazing. Last night I had the most intimate time with [spouse name here]. It was crazy. I tell you, I have never experienced anything like that before!"

Okay, that would be weird. *Whoa! Way too much information.* You'd probably suddenly feel like the room was way too small and way too warm. Your face would probably show the shock: eyes wide, eyebrows lifted, jaw dropped, or a little smirk of amazement. Not sure how to respond you might think, *Did he or she just say that?*

But wait a minute. Take a second and think about the actual statement. The words, I mean. In a conversation this could very well be an adult way of insinuating sexual interaction, which is why we would probably have the reaction described. When we talk about being *intimate* in Western culture we are usually referring to a sexual interaction. But if we look at the word without cultural connotations attached, it isn't necessarily limited in this way. There is way more to the word *intimacy* than just sexual interaction. Much more, in fact.

In this chapter I want to discuss the pursuit of intimacy during the college-age years, and I want to make sure we are looking beyond sexual encounters. The topic of intimacy certainly includes sex and dating for people between ages eighteen and twenty-five, and we will begin this chapter by discussing this aspect of relationships for them. But there is much more depth to relationships that we need to explore in this chapter. Relationships are a critical aspect for college-age people as they discover who they are as individuals. But the relational connections in this younger generation are likely different than what you experienced at this age stage. In some ways you will find they are much more in-depth and intentional—in other ways, well, not so much.

Let's begin with a couple of distinctions between older generations and this younger one when it comes to guy-girl relationships.

DATING EVOLUTION—AVOIDING THE DTR

Dating someone used to be a formal process. When you asked someone out on a date, it was an intentional decision to get to know one another. It showed there was some interest and usually potential for it to go somewhere, potentially marriage. People might have courted each other in groups of friends for a time. If they discovered they liked each other more than friends they would have a conversation where they would define the relationship (otherwise known as a DTR). Typically, if both parties felt the same, they would be titled as girlfriend and boyfriend by the end of this dialogue. They were dating, going steady, or officially in a relationship. And this usually happened fairly early in their interactions. The desire to find a potential mate was part of the initial attraction and the ongoing pursuit of the relationship.

The process is different today, not for everyone but certainly for the majority. In recent years there has been a significant shift when it comes to dating. A rapidly increasing number of college students have placed a high value on noncommittal relationships. This is the thing to do. Sure, many still have exclusive relationships, but as a whole the college-age culture leans toward noncommittal ones.

Girls generally pursue relationships for the status it brings. Having a connection with a boy, especially one who can boost their self-esteem in some way, can be a major motivator. For guys, the pursuit for relational connections with girls during the high school and college-age years is undoubtedly centered in sexuality. Their hormones in full force, they now pursue these relationships out of a desire to fulfill their sexual desires.

You might ask someone, "Do you have a boyfriend?" and get a resounding, "No." However, this doesn't mean she isn't dating someone as you might think of it. In fact, there might be a guy she's been hanging out with, possibly even sleeping with for months now. They're just not making it official.

When we think of dating, we typically think of the nice night out for dinner and a movie. But college dating doesn't even necessarily mean going out on actual dates anymore. Students have told me repeatedly that's not what they think about at all. Official going out dates still happen, but dating has become more about hanging out in the dorm, or watching a movie, or getting wasted together. Terms such as "we're seeing each other" and "we've hooked up a few times" have replaced traditional phrases such as "girlfriend and boyfriend" or "going steady." These new terms are preferred because they carry less committal connotations.

Hook up is the term of choice today and can mean a variety of things, but it always entails some type of physical interaction. Not rushing the responsibilities of marriage and child rearing, college-age people prefer hooking up versus officially dating someone. College-age people are in one of the most sexually active stages of life from a physiological standpoint, but aren't necessarily looking for a mate. What used to be reserved for committed relationships has drifted into sexual encounters with no strings attached. Of course some get more emotionally tied than others, but in general this is a sociological shift embraced by more and more of this generation. Hooking up doesn't have to mean having intercourse, nor does it mean it will lead to a committed relationship. It's a very general term that can mean anything from kissing to oral sex to sexual intercourse.

Mixed-sex dorms with unrestricted access and free-flowing alcohol have left few if any obstacles to a hookup. In other words, hookups are common. And this is true not only at secular schools. It happens with people of faith too—on conservative Christian college campuses. It's an age-stage thing, not a secular versus religious one. I know plenty of Christian people who serve in their churches, are reading Scripture daily, praying—and having sexual interactions periodically with different people. The mixture of desires is intense and confusing, but the lack of commitment makes it all seem a bit easier to manage.

Some psychologists suggest the lack of commitment to exclusive relationships among college students may be a result of delayed maturation. College-age people think about adult life much later now and feel nowhere close to being ready for marriage. So they don't want to commit to any one person or relationship but instead want to explore and enjoy different aspects of life. But they still want to "have fun" or get their "needs met."

More and more college students are saying that their avoidance of monogamy is a result of trying to balance all facets of life for the first time. They're trying to balance their academics, social life, independence, and self-discovery all for the first time. There is less structure in their lives in this stage. They're trying to figure it all out, and adding a committed relationship into the mix is just another thing they would need to balance.

And more open relationships with the opposite sex allows them to focus on themselves rather than having to think about another. The majority of their friends are not seriously dating someone during the first few years after high school, so there's no pressure to find a significant other. Everyone is preoccupied with friends and figuring out what establishing themselves looks like, so long-term relationships aren't top priority. However, the pressures tend to increase after college graduation and toward the end of the college-age years. Whether it's an internal instinct or external pressure, most begin to feel like it's time to be an adult, which includes a desire for a more committed relationship. They become more open to exclusive ones. They have thought through who they are, have discovered more of what they want, are ready to give up some of their selfish focus, and feel like they can handle a serious relationship.

As you can tell there is often a high level of complexity in guy-girl relationships during these years. It would be impossible to have a chapter on relationships without articulating some of the generational distinctions in this area of life. These may look different than your own dating experience, and you may not agree. But these guiding forces are important to understand. As shallow as hookups might be, relationships for this age stage are not.

FORMS AND LIMITATIONS TO INTIMACY

Relationships in general play a vital role in the development of self. The more intimate they are, the stronger influence they are in the formation process. Again, sexual interaction is a part of intimacy, but it's certainly not limited to that. There are actually four kinds of intimacy we can experience. Sometimes a relationship will involve all four kinds, sometimes only one or two. But each kind of intimacy meets a specific type of need for belonging.

    1. Spiritual. This type of intimacy is often the easiest to find because we tend to gravitate toward those who share our spiritual beliefs. Despite a variety of differences in personality, an immediate level of intimacy happens when we discover someone shares our brand of spirituality. College-age people often initiate relationships based on this one aspect of intimacy, making it a kind of front door to lifelong relationships.

2. *Intellectual.* This kind of intimacy suggests that two people have common interests in fields such as culture, politics, hobbies, morality, and ethics. Like spiritual intimacy, intellectual intimacy often leads to quick connections. A simple conversation can initiate an immediate level of intimate connection.

3. *Physical.* Physical intimacy speaks of anything physically oriented: touching, hand holding, snuggling, hugging, kissing, or sexual activity. It implies that we've made a mutual agreement with someone else about sharing personal space—we're allowing and even welcoming another person to be physically close to us. That agreement alone can be a sign that other kinds of intimacy are present in the relationship—but it doesn't dictate that.

4. *Emotional.* This type of intimacy is a little more complex and much more subjective than physical intimacy. For a relationship to have emotional intimacy, both people have to be willing to disclose their deepest thoughts, feelings, and beliefs. But the thoughts and feelings and beliefs that create intimacy come from a person's awareness of themselves. In order for emotional intimacy to occur, each person needs to have developed a certain amount of personal identity. Emotional intimacy also requires trust, which takes time and a willingness to be vulnerable with others.

Why do I mention all this? Outside of the physical, each type of intimacy calls for a level of maturity that the majority of college-age people are still developing. There are always exceptions, and I often see those in spiritual intimacy—there are times when I am blown away at the development and conviction of the college-age people I encounter. But the desire for intimacy is present even while the development process is taking place. The challenge for college-age people comes in learning how to maturely find and nurture the kind of intimate relationships they crave. Without knowing it, they can be unintentionally sabotaging intimacy with people. In fact, hook-ups can rob and potentially thwart their discovery of true intimacy.

INTIMACY ISSUES

Regardless of age we all struggle with some aspects of intimacy. The following issues are common to us all to some degree, but seem to be more obvious and possibly more exaggerated challenges for college-age individuals:

Lack of boundaries.

Without going into a whole explanation of relationship boundaries, let me use the most obvious example of boundary confusion. We can see this issue in opposite sex friendships with those in this stage of life. Two people can be friends, hang out in groups, study together, and go to the movies. They might even talk for hours at times. Without realizing it, one of them crosses from *friend* to *significant other* in the mind of the other person.

College-age women especially get confused and hurt when they realize the guy they've been growing closer to isn't actually interested in being more than friends. They can't understand how a guy can be so emotionally and intellectually intimate without wanting to take the relationship deeper. But men can end up just as confused. They don't know what they did wrong. They tried to

be a good friend and had no idea their friend had other expectations. The issue that comes up is primarily one of boundaries. Both
parties lack the experience to know how to draw appropriate lines
around what a relationship is and what it isn't. Relational tension
and drama crashes in, often breaking the intimacy they once had.

Lack of self-knowledge.

Intimacy happens when two people are able to disclose who they
are to one another. This requires them to first know who they are,
what they want, and what they don't want. This maturity comes
over time and through many exposures and experiences. Intimacy
often comes to a halt because few college-age people know themselves as well as they think they do. They're constantly processing new ideas and experiences, which means their opinions and
beliefs change almost hourly. Consequently, they often contradict
themselves on a regular basis. This inconsistency impedes intimacy.
College-age people aren't able to offer a true and trustworthy self
to a relationship because they haven't found that self yet. The constant change and unpredictability can create frustration and tension
in relationships, which can make true intimacy hard to come by.

Struggle to trust.

Intimacy requires honest communication and vulnerability. But
for college-age people, trust in others' honesty and motives can
be difficult to find—at least initially. They're beginning to realize
many of their high school relationships were convenient, strategic,
or manipulative in some way. From friends to parents, high school
relationships were primarily about the benefits to themselves.
And now, because of their stronger abstract-thinking capabilities,
college-age people also realize they may have been the victim of
someone else's manipulation. Once they've come to this point,
they can become wary of letting themselves be vulnerable with
others. And if they can't trust someone, they can't build intimacy.

Mixtures of disclosure.

This rude awakening to the manipulative power of relationships has another ripple effect that inhibits intimacy. College-age people are able to pick and choose what they reveal about themselves— and what they hold back. They might reveal part of themselves in one relationship and a different part of themselves in another. Technology increases the opportunities to do this as they may play around with different aspects of themselves and different identities on various social networking sites. They can portray themselves any way they want, and can have a tendency to share different sides of themselves on different sites. At its core, this behavior is not so different from previous generations. Prior to the plethora of online platforms, we used to portray ourselves differently in different relational contexts—from work to home to church to neighbors. We could be different people too—just not online.

This mixture of disclosure has at least two unhealthy results. The first issue is that this tendency to only disclose part of themselves in any one relationship gives college-age people the illusion of intimate relationships where intimacy is not really present. Because they think they have deep connections already, they never learn how to wholly reveal themselves to any one person. And without learning how to completely disclose themselves in the context of one relationship, they risk never experiencing real intimacy. I've seen this more times than I can count. This isn't necessarily intentional or manipulative on the part of the younger person, but it is dangerous. Everyone involved can think they have holistic intimacy, but none actually do. There are parts of intimacy present, but a deep intimacy is never reached because the relationship doesn't have full disclosure.

The second problem is that this mixture of disclosure cheats the person's friends out of the intimacy *they* want in the relationship. They think they're getting something they're not—a true, honest friendship. Whether they're on the giving end or the receiving end of incomplete disclosure, college-age people often find themselves unknowingly accepting a poor substitute for real intimacy.

Fear of betrayal.

This issue is less an age-stage problem than a human condition problem. College-age people have lived long enough to have been hurt. Whether it was a dating relationship that ended badly, a friendship that fell apart, or a relationship with parents that shattered in some way, the heartbreak that comes with betrayal lasts a long time. That pain creates fear, and that fear creates a huge barrier to intimacy.

The desire for intimacy among college-age people drives them to make all kinds of decisions and changes. Left alone to navigate the rough waters of relationships, they can easily capsize.

MOTIVATIONS FOR INTIMACY

This stage of life is a highly social stage. Relationships are vital and are pursued with vigor. It's in the context of relationships that the mind is expanded and the self is defined. Despite the challenges they might face in obtaining authentic and holistic intimacy, college-age people can't survive without relationships, so the pursuit continues and lessons are learned along the way.

Relationships play a huge role in the formation of personal convictions. The more someone gets to know another's thoughts and convictions, the more it affects his own thinking and beliefs. This overflow of convictions into the lives of others includes a wide variety of topics, including beliefs about God, mankind, sex, marriage, morality, and child rearing. During the college-age stage of life, the influence of relationships has moved beyond situational peer pressure to drink or try drugs. The influence of relationships in this age stage moves from behavioral to formational.

It's natural for college-age people to experience the process of *differentiation and integration* in the context of relationships (see chapter seven under the discussion of Explorers for a refresher). They will look at and critique the characteristics in other individuals, including friends, parents, coworkers, pastors, speakers, or homeless people. Because college-age people are constantly examining who they are as individuals, they are looking to see who others are. This starts in relationships. College-age people will differentiate between characteristics they respect and desire and those they dislike and don't want.

Of course, they can't verbally articulate that this is what they're doing. But it's evident even during minimal encounters with college-age people. As twentysomethings eventually try to integrate those characteristics they respect and desire into their own lives, their relationships move from an influence to a powerful former of their identities. Additionally, and often in much more complex ways, they begin to see that sometimes the characteristics they don't like in others actually exist inside of themselves as well. Through this process, college-age people become much more aware of who they are, assess what they are learning, and begin to adjust accordingly.

This is why relational intimacy is pursued. The better they know someone else, the more they learn about themselves. It's why twentysomethings constantly seek relational connection. Some people are more introverted than others, of course, but in general even they feel a deep desire for intimacy.

Relational intimacy brings new thoughts in areas of religion, philosophy, and the sciences. It brings fresh perspective on values and morality. It expands their minds to new horizons. And all these combine into a powerful influence in their lives.

CRITIQUING OTHERS TO SEEKING PERSPECTIVE

College-age people will take conversation to a whole other level with someone they truly value and trust. This happens when they move away from analyzing what they observe in other people to seeking other people's opinions about themselves. For instance, I've had this happen frequently with interns. It's not that they stop thinking about who I am or the characteristics I possess, but at some point they put that on hold. Instead, the intern wants to know what I think of him or her. I get questions such as, "What comes to your mind when you think about me?" or "Who do you see me being?" I've also heard more specific perspectives, including, "What would you say my areas of strength are?" or "What character issues do you think I need to work on the most?"

These questions clue us in to a number of things. First, they show an initiative in self-discovery and reveal an ongoing internalization prior to asking. They are now putting their finger on some aspects of themselves and are looking for affirmation of those thoughts.

Second, these questions show trust in the person they are asking—trust in that person's opinion and trust that the person will give an honest answer. College-age people who are asking these types of questions are in a process of honestly assessing who they are. They will only ask the opinion of those they feel will help them in this authentic critique.

Third, these questions reveal abstract thinking abilities operating in full force. These twentysomethings are comparing their own definition of themselves with the perceptions of others. It doesn't mean they have everything figured out, but they are close to landing on who they are. They are fairly confident in their own skin at this point and have processed through characteristics in others. The formation of identity will, of course, be an ongoing learning process for the rest of their lives. But the importance they are placing on it now might save them some real heartache later.

Unfortunately many people jump into a job or relationship and often unknowingly end up substituting that thing for who they really are. Then at an older age, when there is much more at stake and more people can be negatively affected, people withdraw from their commitments blaming the fact that they've lost themselves. They now feel the need to forgo their responsibilities to others in order to find out who they are. You might know of this firsthand.

I hope you can see how this seemingly aimless search during the college-age years is actually not as aimless as it may seem on the surface. Yes, college-age people can tend to float through life. Sure, the time it takes them to sift through who they are and what they want can be far longer than anyone would like it to be. It might seem like all they do is hang out with friends or jump from one relationship to another without committing anywhere. But there is a vital search for self driving them.

THE PARENT TRAP

If you are a parent there is a reality you must be aware of: Your child desires a relationship with you. There might be some obstacles for you here. Most children have crept away from you relationally, at least to some degree, throughout middle and high school. They moved from never wanting to leave your side to wanting to be dropped off two blocks away to now pursuing relationships with other people who will help them find out who they are apart from you. But make no mistake about it, they can never fully separate. They never stop needing their parents. It's just that we need to adapt as parents.

Regardless of what you may feel or what your child may have said last week, a relationship with you is more than a *need*. It's a *desire*. The truth is most children don't want to separate either. You are your child's parent. That is a space nobody else in the world can fill. And no matter how broken your relationship might be at this moment, know that your child probably wishes it wasn't.

I talked with one mother of a college sophomore who was dealing with some insecurities in her relationship with her daughter. At times she felt secure, but other times she felt terribly disconnected. There were times her phone rang late in the evening, and her daughter had a life question. She felt great because her daughter actually wanted and needed to talk to her. But then there were long periods of time when her daughter only called asking for money or cut short a visit home. Those were the times the mother felt insecure. *Is my daughter withdrawing? What is she thinking about? Who is influencing her?* These are scary questions, especially at this stage of life when a mom is questioning her role in her daughter's life. It's a scary realization that a mother doesn't even know the majority of people who are relationally influencing her daughter.

But this mother sat back and patiently waited for the phone to ring. She didn't want to hover and push her daughter away. She didn't want to become an annoyance.

I also sat down with her daughter. I never shared the feelings of her mom. I simply asked questions. And without even knowing it the daughter gave some great insights into the relational tension her mom felt. Here are a few things the daughter wished her mom understood:

- The disconnect was not because the daughter didn't love or value her mom. She was simply feeling the need to find out who she was individually.

- The daughter felt like she already knew what her mom would say with most topics, so she didn't feel the need to ask as often. It's not that she didn't think about what her mom would say. She simply wanted to know what other people thought too.

- The daughter felt that her mom's advice was biased. She didn't blame her mom for this, but she felt like her mom couldn't give her totally objective advice.

These insights don't erase the tension, but they can bring a sense of comfort to parents. Of course it's scary to realize your child is out there trying to find herself and you are totally out of control. But it can be helpful to know that what you're experiencing is a part of growing up—not a personal rejection. It's just an age-stage thing—and ultimately a healthy aspect of life.

Try not to get caught in the trap of enviously looking to other parents and the relationships they have with their kids. Most of the time your perception of someone else's relationship doesn't match reality. Finally, regardless of how close a college-age person is with her parents, there are always things her parents will never know. But God knows. We can always pray. We can always ask questions. And we can always be there when the phone rings. And that type of stability is what today's college-age kids truly need.

CHAPTER 10

NAVIGATING INTERGENERATIONAL RELATIONSHIPS

Intergenerational relationships sound great. I hear from people all the time who desire to develop intergenerational relationships and live in contexts where they are the norm. I talk to people from different generations who think the give and take between generations sounds positive and ideal.

Unfortunately I also find it doesn't take long for most to revert to a pessimistic view that intergenerational relationships are extremely idealistic and can never actually happen in our culture or churches. There are seemingly too many obstacles to overcome in order for relationships between generations to work. But I argue that living in and helping cultivate relationships with people of different generations is not only possible, it is happening. And I want to help you continue the trend.

I have extremely introverted friends who have developed intimate relationships with people very different from them. I know some adults who have overcome incredible feelings of intimidation to become secure in healthy relationships with younger people.[1] It wasn't always easy. Bridging their world with a college-age person's required my friends to make adjustments.

Simply desiring a closer relationship with someone of a different generation is a good start, but there has to be more than desire. There is a balancing act to learn if you are going to effectively navigate and cultivate these relationships. You must be able to intentionally pursue without overstructuring your relationship.

You need to be humble and understand that you can also learn a lot from younger people. And you need to honor diverse ways of communication. Understanding these balances is critical in order to connect your world to a younger person's.

INTENTIONALITY WITHOUT OVERSTRUCTURING

If you are part of an older generation, you probably have ingrained into your thinking that you need to establish your purpose and goals for your relationship with younger people. You want to be intentional. Maybe you are a parent who wants to connect simply to understand and help your child. Maybe the reason you've read this book is that you simply want to be a deeper part of your child's life and are looking for ways to rekindle or navigate your relationship. Or maybe you work with college-age people and want to be more effective in relating to and mentoring them.

Whatever the case I encourage you to recognize the fact that you have some type of agenda based on your own desires. I'm not saying it's a bad agenda; in fact, I assume it's a good one. But be honest in recognizing that you're trying to accomplish something. If you feel like that agenda is not getting accomplished, you will have a tendency to either withdraw from the relationship because your expectations aren't being met or restructure your relationship in order to make it happen. When you meet with a college-age person, you have reasons why you took time out of your busy schedule to do it. You want it to be purposeful. You have limited time and therefore want your time to be meaningful. I understand completely.

But you must be careful of an agenda. Your desires may be noble, but relationships built on any self-seeking agendas don't last long. This is especially true when relating to college-age people today.

To effectively navigate a relationship with a college-age person you should only have one agenda: to get to know that person.

Get to know who they are, what they personally desire, what they think about, care for, and want to pursue in life. As a parent you might think you already know most of these things. You might, but things are constantly changing at this age, and I'd encourage you to consider the possibility that you don't know as much as you think you do.

In other words, regardless of how well you may know someone, your relationship should be about them, not you. Self-focused agendas, regardless of what they are, always lower the ceiling of relationships. But when we take the focus off of our own desires and expectations and put the focus on others we open it to limitless possibility.

Do you have a person in your life who always leaves you feeling encouraged, regardless of the time or location? Ever thought about why that is?

I'm convinced it's because that person is genuinely interested in you. She doesn't have an agenda. She doesn't try to over-structure your times together. She asks questions about *your* life. She is interested in what is happening with you. She gives her opinions only when asked—as a result you probably ask more frequently. You have no questions about her motivations because she's proven to you over time that she cares about you and wants what's best for you.

If you want to navigate a relationship with a college-age person, you need to be this source of encouragement for him or her. To make sure you can be, I encourage you to think about the following questions:

- In relationships do you tend to talk about yourself or your own opinions a lot? Or are you able to let others do most of the talking, at least at first? The second approach will be much more effective in building a relationship with a college-age person.

- When someone talks about an experience she had, do you tend to feel the need to share how *you* can personally relate to that issue? Or do you ask more questions about what that experience was like for her? If it's the latter, then you'll be on your way to a deep and meaningful relationship.

- Do you have a genuine interest in what other people desire? If so, you will be able to genuinely help guide a college-age person toward a life direction.

- Do you honestly respect the fact that others don't always place as high of a value on the same things you do? If so, there is no limit to the depth of your relationship!

- Do you desire to objectively help other people move in the direction *they* desire? If so, you will frequently be asked for counsel by college-age people.

LEARNING WITH HUMILITY

College-age people need people like you in their lives. But you could use them too. My friend Laverne is eighty-seven years old, and she's one of my heroes in life. My favorite way to describe her is "just an old saint who loves Jesus." I love talking with her. She's full of so much life, and wisdom always seems to leak out in such simple and bottom-line statements. I love talking with her because she genuinely cares and is always praying for me. I'm always encouraged by my times with her.

It's also fun to see that she absolutely loves hanging out with younger people. In fact, she says she would rather hang out with younger people than anyone else. That's quite a statement from someone her age. Laverne has told me many times that relationships with younger people bring her life. That's interesting to me because Laverne is already so full of life herself. It's life-giving for me to spend time with her. It sometimes surprises me that it is mutual. But it proves that these relationships always seem to go both ways. You probably notice that too. When you sincerely seek to serve and help other people, don't you often feel like you get more out of it than they do?

Laverne has told me what she enjoys most about college-age people is their passion, sense of idealism, and energy. And this eighty-seven-year-old frequently tells me she is learning! And she is a learner of people. The individuals she mentors are different from her in a thousand ways, and that's what she loves. She wants to know what they think about and the conclusions they are coming to. She's humble. She doesn't try to get them to embrace her generational values. Laverne has her values that she will never budge on, but she's always interested in "broadening her horizons" (that's a phrase she uses frequently). These characteristics are precisely what make her attractive to younger people.

Laverne never comes into a conversation with any other agenda than to enjoy a conversation with you. I think she has tapped into a secret of the college-age generation: The more we open our ears to what a younger generation has to say, the more they ask us to speak into their lives.

Navigating intergenerational relationships isn't difficult if we follow the example of this old saint. If we can, building a relationship with a college-age person is not only possible, it's simple.

Christian college-age people are desperate for an experience they know is divine. They don't just want to know about God, they want to experience him. Many, not all, want to walk with God daily, be a part of what he's doing, and be used by him. Sure, experience-based pursuits can be incredibly dangerous if they are separated from truth. But experiencing God can also be rooted in truth. And this is what I find many college-age people seeking. This is also another reason they connect with Laverne and others like her, who experience God daily. Laverne is always reading

Scripture and praying, and her authentic faith and intimacy with God are apparent to everyone.

Unfortunately I find a lack of older adults who authentically experience God daily. Many, if you ask them directly, have a hard time pointing out anything specific they feel like God is teaching them or working on in their lives today. Few actively pray for others. Far too many can't explain their own testimony of how and why they personally decided to follow Jesus—and fewer can explain why they still do today. I hear more and more pastors talking about how the adults in their churches lack intimacy with God on a daily basis. Many know about the Bible, but they don't know God. They may be able to regurgitate information, but they lack experience of living it out.

Such disengaged faith is extremely unattractive to college-age people—repulsive, in fact. There's no life, no passion, no sense of mission, and no humility in a dependence on God. When college-age people have faith, they want it to be authentic—they want to live it out. They want their lives to match what their mouths are saying or what their brain understands. This can get a bit twisted at times, but generally speaking people in this stage of life are passionate about their faith—maybe more than those in any other stage as a whole. Witnessing such passion is one of the beautiful things about connecting with them!

If you're someone who knows about the Bible, is rooted in church culture, but are not experiencing God daily I encourage you to do just one thing: Spend time with a college-age Christian. Sure, they will have weaknesses, issues, and inconsistencies—we all do. But if you desire to revive the experiential side of your faith, spending time with a younger person can be just the thing to ignite and inspire your own faith. Sure, twentysomethings might be idealistic and a little nuts, but their passion and desire to know God will rub off. I know this from firsthand experience.

If you desire to build relationships with college-age people, having a balance of knowing information and humbly living it out will be a magnet. It's part of what draws people to Laverne. We all love to be around the Lavernes of the world. Now, if we can just work at *being* the Lavernes of the world we will be well on our way to bridging the generational chasms.

DIVERSE COMMUNICATION

I was talking to a college-age guy about a recent job change he made. I knew he had applied and interviewed for the position, but I didn't know how things had worked out. We sat down for lunch, and he started talking about the job change as if I were already aware of it. I let him know I had known nothing about the change until that moment, but I was happy for him. He was totally shocked. The look on his face was not feeling bad that he hadn't informed me earlier; he was legitimately shocked that I didn't already know.

"Well how would I have known? We haven't talked in a couple weeks," I asked.

He looked at me with bewilderment and said, "I posted it in a Facebook update."

Well, there you go! How could I have missed that?!

It was a moment of generational disconnect. He couldn't believe I hadn't been keeping up with his life on Facebook, and I couldn't believe he expected me to. The world he has grown up in has a communication norm that mine did not. I utilize technology in many ways, but the ways I communicate with others are different than this twentysomething. I would never assume someone knows about my current situation simply because I posted something on Facebook. In fact, I'm surprised when people bring up things I have posted. I simply don't expect it. But my college-age friends expect nothing less.

Later that evening I scrolled through that guy's Facebook page. Sure enough, there was the update. This served as yet another reminder that in order to relate to younger people I need to learn to communicate in diverse ways. There are clearly new expectations.

I can question if this friend can relate to anyone in person, but the fact is he can. He just relates in diverse ways, and technology is a major part of that.

I'm not suggesting you stalk college-age people in cyberspace, nor am I suggesting we constantly check everyone's Facebook status so we don't look stupid. But we have to accept that the worlds we are used to are in fact different. We can work harder at recognizing college-age people's forms of communication as effective and legitimate. And hopefully they can begin to see the value of the face-to-face encounters we are accustomed to.

Don't be surprised if you find that college-age people feel comfortable commenting on a blog, but very uncomfortable sharing their thoughts in person, especially when it involves any type of confrontation. But instead of criticizing their generation for this, we can help them develop interpersonal skills through our relationships in a few different ways.

First, we can model what it looks like to communicate face to face. If we have something we want to tell them, we can make a point to sit down personally rather than texting or even calling. This isn't necessarily better than a Facebook post, but we can model the positives of communicating certain information in person, especially if it's personal or confrontational. The critical balance is making sure you model the beauty of physical presence in relationships and to do this *without* dishonoring technological forms of communication.

Second, we can make sure we communicate that our identity is always within the context of real-life relationships. We might be able to communicate through online technologies, but we live life with real people every day. We can make sure they know how much we appreciate this type of accountability in our own lives and how much we like having to be consistent in our everyday lives because people see how we live. In doing so, there is no need to belittle online communication. In fact we don't even need to bring that up. Instead, we can simply promote personal relationships, the accountability they bring, and the joy of sitting across a table from someone as you talk about the happenings of your lives.

Perhaps the key point in this is simply to spend time with them individually. The deeper their personal relationships are, especially with people who are older and have more life experience, the more grounding younger people will have. An online presence can give anyone a *sense* of identity, but it doesn't provide belonging in our daily lives. I firmly believe that many people seek an online identity because they lack quality relationships in everyday life. You can provide that for those who struggle with this!

DEEPER THAN A CONVERSATION

The people who have the greatest sense of belonging in the world are those who are grounded in multiple intimate and truly meaningful relationships. Take the workplace, for example. We can absolutely love what we *do* in our job, but if we don't have good relationships with the people we work alongside, we won't have a sense of belonging where we work. The opposite is also true. We can hate what we *do* in our job, but if we have deep and meaningful connections with the people we work with, we can have a sense of belonging.

The pursuit of intimacy has much larger implications in the lives of college-age people than we might think. It goes much deeper than a desire for social interactions or friendship. It's even deeper than a longing to overcome feelings of isolation or detachment. It's a quest for identity in connection and community—the kind of relationship I believe is one of the hallmarks of the Christian faith. It might be better summarized in the term *belonging*.

In fact, if we lose a sense of belonging in the church (meaning the people), we lose our identity in the world. College-age Christians are seeking a place in the world, but in order to truly land on that identity they need to be connected to people in the church—people just like you.

Belonging is found in the context of three relationships: our relationship with ourselves, our relationship with other people, and our relationship with God. We lose our sense of belonging in the world if any one of these relationships are lacking a foundation. When any of these are out of whack, we never totally feel comfortable. Show me a person who desires more relational connections, and I'll show you a person who is struggling to feel like he belongs. Show me a person who is questioning everything about God, and I'll show you a person who is struggling to find belonging. Show me a person who is not quite sure who she is, and I'll show you a person who doesn't feel like she belong yet.

Of course, many college-age people are unsettled in all three areas. They are still figuring out who they are. They are seeking intimate connection. And they are still trying to figure out what they believe about God and faith. I guess I could say if you show me a college-age person, I'll show you a person seeking belonging.

You are needed for much more than a conversation. You can fill a meaningful and significant role in the life of a younger person. You can be a part of providing a sense of belonging to someone who desperately seeks it. If you are willing to pay the price of time and get to know a college-age person as a learner with no other agenda, you are going to be part of something much bigger than a conversation. And if you are willing to mesh your world with theirs by properly navigating these relationships, you will also have an even greater sense of belonging yourself.

May your humility be the bridge that brings two lives, two generations, two worlds together.

APPENDIX A

PRACTICAL NOTES FOR CHURCH LEADERS

Your role as a leader of college-age people in a church context is unique. You serve in a place of great challenges, but even greater potential. This whole book is written with you in mind, but I wanted to provide you with a quick-and-easy reference point for some of the main ideas that relate specifically to the role you play in the lives of twenysomethings.

BIG PICTURE RESPONSE

As you know from experience, and have read in the first few chapters of this book, this life stage can be highly complex. And ministry to college-age people requires a lot of time spent with people on an individual basis. It's one thing to set up a church service musically and aesthetically geared toward younger people. This can be a great and beneficial addition to a ministry, but it cannot be viewed as the ending point. You can pour a ton of time and resources into this and still never get to the heart of what these people need or desire. Just because you have a thousand people sitting in a room, doesn't mean they are connecting in the necessary ways.

I know because I found this out the hard way.[1]

College-age people need more than a program to go to. They need, and want, people to spend time with them. The overall structure that's appropriate and most effective with college-age people might include some type of large(r) gathering specifically designed for them. But the sustainability and life-changing nature of a ministry to twentysomethings is typically found in providing a deeper connection to your church, through specific relationships with older adults in your church. It's in the context of relationships that people gain a sense of belonging. It's there that true identity formation can take place. Imagine the impact older adults who consistently model Christ-like characteristics can have when they invest personally in the lives of younger people. College-age people are going to go through differentiation and integration anyway . . . we might as well invest a great deal of time pointing them to people with characteristics worth adopting.

LIFE DIRECTION

In chapter five we talked through the complexities of pursuing a direction in life and finding a life vocation. You can play a key role in helping college-age people through that process. Find the accountants or doctors or grocery store clerks in your church who view their jobs as their mission fields. Ask these folks to spend time with college-age people. Encourage them to share their perspective on the direction they've chosen in life, and to show how any vocational path can be purposeful and Kingdom focused.

ENTITLEMENT, EGO, AND THE PURSUIT OF PLEASURE

Entitlement is a widespread generational issue for today's twentysomethings. Chapter six goes into detail about ways this character issue often shows up in this generation. A practical response for you as a leader might be something as simple as asking yourself one question: "Do I tend to value how the gifts of others can be used in my ministry more than I value them growing in Christ-like character?" It's not that a person's gifts can't be used while at the same time working on building charater. The two can clearly take place simultaneously. But this is a heart question for you, personally.

The tendency to meet with people for what we can get out of them is always a temptation in ministry. We get busy, feel the pressure of logistics and numbers. And our time with people ends up being far more about getting stuff done than becoming like Christ in our character. We have a heart for their spiritual maturity, for sure. But if we're not careful we neglect digging into the deeper issues of character development. When we do this, we are enabling the young people we work with to view the development of their gifts and abilities as being more important than the development of character. One of the most important lessons we can teach people of this generation is that God often uses character more than gifts. Gifts might get people places, but character keeps them there. From a very practical perspective, I'd encourage you to step back in a posture of prayer and introspectively determine where your focus is, and where you'd like it to be.

GUIDING THE SEARCH FOR SELF

In chapter seven I wrote through five different stages people go through in determining their identity. If you are involved with college-age people, spend some time figuring out where individuals are in this process. What stage(s) are they in? What are some practical questions you can ask them to help them continue progressing through these stages?[2] Are there specific things you can personally expose them to or help them experience that would assist them in becoming more self-aware?

THE PURSUIT OF PERSONAL CONVICTION

The process college-age people go through to determine their own beliefs and convictions apart from those of their parents was the focus of chapter eight. In your ministry, and specifically in your teaching, are you addressing this process? Do you recognize the reality that college-age people want and need to process

through things for themselves? Or, do you find yourself stunt-
ing the thought process by constantly explaining the conclusions
you've come to personally?

Your conclusions may be right on. But the point is that they
are *your* conclusions. If we are interested in guiding the thought
processes of college-age people instead of simply indoctrinating
them, we will begin to teach differently. Not only will we address
the questions they're already asking, but we will also stretch their
thinking to embrace even more questions. I've found that if we
are the ones that initiate the asking of questions then we are most
often the ones they come back to as they try to formulate their
own conclusions. If, however, all we do is articulate our conclusions
and never stretch their thinking, they will tend to go elsewhere for
answers too—it's their way of figuring it out for themselves.

EVOLUTION AND ROLE OF RELATIONSHIPS

It's an obvious point to say that the people we are close to have
a great deal of influence on us. But in the church we sometimes
fail to take that to its natural conclusion: If college-age people
lose relational connection with other maturing Christians, they
naturally lose Christian influence in their lives. Consequently they
are inevitably influenced by what they are close to—which can
lead them away from truth. Once again, I believe the best way
to keep this from happening is to develop a ministry structure
where a percentage of your time is focused on cultivating relationships between people in your church and college-age people. The
bottom line is that I believe if leaders would pour as much time
into relationships as programs and events, our effectiveness would
increase greatly. There is a role for both events and relationships in
our churches, but events without sustainable relational connections
are rarely worth the time, energy, and money they require.

FINDING COMMON GROUND AND BUILDING BRIDGES

When we think of leaders we often think of "type A" people who are comfortable in front of people, can teach in larger formats, and are able to convince others to be a part of what they lead. This type of dynamic and persuasive leader can be very effective. But we can't let this stereotype limit our concept of leadership. In fact, for our conversation, I'd suggest it's not even the image of leadership we should begin with.

A new breed of leader needs to be considered when we think of ministry to college-age people. When we need leaders for our middle school ministry we look for characteristics in people that fit the uniqueness of that ministry. The same should be true of ministry to college-age people.

College-age people desire to be a part of a church not just a ministry. A specific ministry can be a starting point, but there's eventually a craving for more. That is where the right kind of people in leadership become crucial.

In order to bring a sense of commonality we need leaders who are already relationally connected to different types of people. They may have friends that are of different generations. They know a single mom, they know parents of preschoolers and they know empty-nesters. These don't have to be intimate lifelong friendships, but the key is they are relationally connected to different types of people in the church. It's these people being involved in the beginning of our ministry that will naturally bridge college-age people to the larger body. Leaders who can naturally provide and encourage those connections between young people and others in the church will be a huge help as you work to build bridges between the generations.

OTHER RESOURCES

And now for my shameless self-promotion section. In all serious-
ness, I do believe these resources have the potential to give you
inspiration as well as practical advice as you minister to college-
age people.

If your church doesn't yet have a ministry to college-age
people and would like some practical help getting started, I would
recommend my recent book, *College Ministry from Scratch: A Practical Guide to Start and Sustain a Successful College Ministry.* This is
a practical guide for how to focus, structure, and measure your
college ministry. It also provides practical advice in all of the daily
facets of your ministry like small groups, working with interns,
putting on retreats, leading mission trips, and figuring out teaching topics.

College Ministry 101: A Guide to Working with 18-25 Year Olds
is another book I've written related to this topic. This book articu-
lates an overall philosophy of ministry, walks through how to dis-
ciple students in areas of identity, meaning, truth, intimacy, and
pursuits of pleasure, as well as providing insights into what and
who the leader of this ministry ought to be.

Finally, I've coauthored a book designed to help individual
Christian adults understand their role in the life of a college-age
person. The book is called, *The Slow Fade: Why You Matter in the
Story of Twentysomethings.* I'd recommend reading this yourself and
giving it out to anyone you think might be interested in personally
investing in the life of a younger person. More resources you can
provide mentors and those working on intergenerational relationships can be found at www.xp3College.org.[3]

PRACTICAL NOTES FOR PARENTS

My job puts me in a position where parents often ask me for advice. I find I am hesitant to give many answers. I prefer to ask questions and guide conversations rather than giving specific advice. I've never parented a college-age person—my girls are still in elementary school. But while I can't speak from personal experience on the parenting side, I can speak from hours spent with parents and their college-age children. I hope the experiences of the many families I've worked with will speak to you and your situation. The recurring themes, issues, desires, heartaches, and joys are all very familiar. In fact, you probably already know everything I am about to say. But I offer these common pressure points and principles as reminders—as a source of help and encouragement for when you face similar situations in your relationships.

IT GETS PERSONAL

Your child will always be your baby. But the days of cribs and strollers and midnight feedings are long gone. (Thank goodness!) And in the place of the child you once had, is a young adult who wants to be seen as not just your child, but as an independent person. Even though they may still be dependent in many ways, your child wants to be treated as an equal rather than a dependent child. As parents we have to recognize that our kids are going to develop their own thoughts, as any person would. This means they will make all the important decisions about their lives apart from us—some, of course sooner than others. I've observed that parents who talk to their college-age children as friends tend to have more influence into their lives. Those who tend to speak as opinionated parents tend to lose influence. That doesn't mean you won't ever be part of a decision-making process, but your child has reached the point where he needs to have the freedom and responsibility to make his own choices. Watching this can be exciting, scary, freeing, and heartbreaking all at once.

The transition can be extra challenging if your kids are still living at home. When they're still under your roof, it's hard not to be involved in every aspect of their lives. I stand by the principle that if you are paying the bills, they still need to obey your rules. But in the interest of maintaining and growing the relationship, I'd encourage you to work hard at stepping back, choosing your battles, and concentrating on moral character issues rather than personal preferences.

The good news is that your child is also at a stage where she begins to view you not only as a parent but as a person. As college-age people begin to learn about themselves they soon realize their parents are human beings as well. These realizations often lead to greater appreciation for you, the parent. As you and your child adapt to these changes, you'll see your interactions begin to move from management to relationship—a wonderful and welcome change for many parents and children. It's not easy, but I've seen that parents who make this transition tend to have closer relationships with their kids.

WANTED!

Your child wants to connect with you. It may not feel that way, but it is true. So true, in fact, that your child may withhold information about her life that she thinks will cause conflict in your relationship. This can naturally cause you to wonder and worry. But let's be honest here, there is a lot you don't know about your kids. They did things in middle school and high school that you know nothing about and never will—and you probably don't want to either. This sounds discouraging, but I point it out as an encouragement: Just because your child doesn't tell you everything, doesn't mean he doesn't want a relationship with you. They want freedom *and* you. Yes, college-age people are likely exploring different aspects of life that they know their parents disagree with. But experience shows me that the parents who work at respecting the space their kids desire instead of pushing and prying, usually end up having closer and more meaningful relationships with their children.

KEEP IT SIMPLE

The college years are a complex time of life. When you feel bewildered, keep it simple. Be a friend. Ask questions. Listen. Be there when they want to talk and don't overuse your freedom to call. Back off on your involvement, but never stop pouring on the love.

ENDNOTES

CHAPTER 2

1. Robin Marantz, "What Is It About Twentysomethings?," *New York Times Magazine* (August 18, 2010).

2. E. H. Erikson, *Childhood and Society* (New York: Norton, 1950).

3. Chap Clark, *Hurt: Inside the World of Today's Teenagers* (Grand Rapids, Mich.: Baker Academic, 2004), 28.

4. "Digest of Education Statistics, 2008," U.S. Department of Education, *National Center for Education Statistics, www.nces. ed.gov.* (April 18, 2011).

5. *Ibid.*

6. "College Enrollment and Work Activity of 2009 High School Graduates," April 27, 2010, *Bureau of Labor Statistics, http:// www.bls.gov/news.release/hsgec.nr0.htm* (April 18, 2011).

7. "Digest of Education Statistics, 2008," U.S. Department of Education, *National Center for Education Statistics, www.nces. ed.gov.* (April 18, 2011).

8. "Integrated Postsecondary Education Data System (IPEDS)," Graduation Rates component, March 2010, Enrollment in Postsecondary Institutions, Fall 2007; Graduation Rates, 2001

and 2004 Cohorts; and Financial Statistics, Fiscal Year 2007. U.S. Department of Education, *National Center for Education Statistics, www.nces.ed.gov.* (April 18, 2011).

9. For more see Godfrey and Matos-Elefonte, "Key Indicators of College Success: Predicting College Enrollment, Persistance, and Graduation," May 14, 2010, *College Board, http://professionals.collegeboard.com* (April 18, 2011).

10. "Digest of Education Statistics, 2009," U.S. Department of Education, *National Center for Education Statistics, www.nces.ed.gov.* (April 18, 2011).

11. Tiffany Ann Johnson. "In a grim post-grad job market, is staying in school your best option?" May 14, 2010, *USAToday College, www.usatodayeducate.com/staging* (April 18, 2011).

12. "Digest of Education Statistics, 2005," U.S. Department of Education, *National Center for Education Statistics, www.nces.ed.gov.* (April 18, 2011).

13. "Digest of Education Statistics, 2008," U.S. Department of Education, *National Center for Education Statistics, www.nces.ed.gov.* (April 18, 2011).

CHAPTER 3

1. Steven Greenhouse, "'Glimmers of Hope' for Grads," May 24, 2010, *New York Times, www.nytimes.com/2010/05/25/business/economy/25gradjobs.html* (April 18, 2011).

2. Arnett, J.J., "Emerging Adulthood: A Theory of Development from the Late Teens through the Twenties.," *American Psychologist*, 55 (May 2000), 469-480.

3. The most recent worldwide research provided by the United Nations for these figures are from 2000. Although these statistics are more than a decade old, the historical trajectory of this trend would suggest they are at least the same, if not higher today. A summary of worldwide statistics for women can be found at *http://www.nationmaster.com/graph/peo_age_at_fir_mar_for_wom-people-age-first-marriage-women#source*. A summary for men can be found at *http://www.nationmaster. com/graph/peo_age_at_fir_mar_for_men-people-age-first-marriage-men*. Figures for European and North American countries come from UN Economic Commission for Europe, Trends in Europe and North America 2001 (UN, NY, 2001). New Zealand figures from Maureen Baker, Families, Labour and Love (Allen & Unwin, Sydney, 2001). Japanese figures from Japan Almanac 1998 (Asahi Shimbun, Tokyo).

4. Paul Taylor and Wendy Wang, "For Millenials, Parenthood Trumps Marriage," March 29, 2011, *www.pewresearch.org* (April 18, 2011).

5. Source: U.S. Bureau of the Census; *www.census.gov. http://www.infoplease.com/ipa/A0005061.html*.

6. "Digest of Education Statistics, 2008," U.S. Department of Education, *National Center for Education Statistics, www.nces. ed.gov*. (April 18, 2011).

7. John Modell, *Into one's own: From Youth to Adulthood in the United States, 1920-1975* (Berkeley: University of California Press, 1989).

8. "Digest of Education Statistics, 2008," Table 188, U.S. Department of Education, *National Center for Education Statistics, www.nces.ed.gov*. (April 18, 2011).

9. It is tough to find more recent research on this particular statistic taken from the National Center for Education Statistics (2002), *http://.nces.ed.gov.* However, the trends documented at *The Network on Transitions to Adulthood, www. transad.pop.upenn.edu/about/index.html,(April 18, 2011),* confirm that this financial dependence is growing, rather than decreasing with time.

10. "Young Workers: A Lost Decade," *AFL-CIO Labor Day Report, www.aflcio.org* (April 18, 2011).

11. The Project On Student Debt, *www.projectonstudentdebt. org.* The facts and analysis for this study are based on the Project on Student Debt's analysis of data from the National Postsecondary Student Aid Study (NPSAS). Conducted by the U.S. Department of Education every four years, NPSAS is a comprehensive nationwide survey designed to determine how undergraduate students and their families pay for college.

12. Sandra Block, "In Debt Before You Start," *USA Today,* June 12, 2006. This report shows that in 2006 the average college senior graduated with $19,000 in debt, but The Project for Student Debt says today approximately 10 percent of students have over $40,000 worth of loans they need to pay back after graduating.

13. Federal Pell Grant Program, U.S. Department of Education, *http://www2.ed.gov/programs.*

14. "Tuition and Fee and Room and Board Charges, 2010–11," *College Board, www.collegeboard.org* (April 18, 2011).

CHAPTER 7

1. James Marcia, "Identity in adolescence," in *Joseph Adelson (Ed.), Handbook of Adolescent Psychology* (New York: Wiley, 1980). Also see James Marcia, "The empirical study of ego identity," in *Harke Bosma, Harold Grotevant & David De Levita (Eds.), Identity and Development* (Newbury Park, Calif.: Sage, 1994).

2. David Elkind, *All Grown Up and No Place to Go: Teenagers in Crisis* (New York: Perseus Books, 1998), 18–22.

3. Jeffrey Jensen Arnett, *Emerging Adulthood: The Winding Road from the Late Teens through the Twenties* (Oxford University Press, 2006). In chapter one, Arnett breaks these influences down into work, school, and love. However, it's not only in love relationships (i.e., dating) where identity is formed. Normal peer relationships also play a huge role and, in some ways, are even more influential.

4. David Elkind, *All Grown Up and No Place to Go: Teenagers in Crisis* (New York: Perseus Books, 1998), 18. Although Elkind doesn't limit this process to college age (late adolescence), he's clear that it's the healthiest way to formulate a sense of identity. He contrasts this stage with a substituted identity. The substituted identity is often formulated, or adapted, because the individual's abstract thinking hasn't yet developed to a point where he can walk through differentiation and integration. This underdevelopment leaves the individual with no choice but to adapt to different atmospheres, which Elkind calls "the development of a patchwork self." It makes sense that this person would be more susceptible to peer pressure because he lacks a sense of identity beyond the atmospheres in which he finds himself. Because this person has yet to think through who he is and how he may be different from others, he substitutes his true identity for that

of his immediate context (i.e., circumstances in which he currently is). In my research, people who think through their identity at the Explorer level are typically college age. I do believe adults can push high school students to think through these issues, but teenagers typically won't on their own. Also, they're less likely to make changes in their lives despite seeing contradictions in them.

CHAPTER 8

1. UCLA has done some research on spirituality in higher education and compiled it in *A National Study of College Students' Search for Meaning and Purpose.* You can find more at www.spirituality.ucla.edu and in the book by Astin, Astin, and Lindholm, *Cultivating the Spirit: How College Can Enhance Students' Inner Lives* (Jossey-Bass, October, 2009).

CHAPTER 10

1. In order to help adults understand their role and importance in the life of younger people I have also coauthored, *The Slow Fade: Why You Matter in the Story of Twentysomethings.* This book differs from this resource in that it is less about the college-age stage of life and more about helping older adults understand how and why they ought to invest into a college-age person. This may be a good next level read for you.

APPENDIX A

1. The first chapter of my book, *College Ministry from Scratch* is devoted to articulating my story of learning this.

2. I provide a ton of practical advice and questions on how to guide this process in chapters 2-6 of my book *College Ministry 101.*

3. At *www.xp3College.org* you will find videos, seminars, and a ton of conversation guides for two people from different generations to go through together. We provide training and understanding for the mentor as well. But these guides bring a balance. First, they give the older adult something to go by in their time with a younger person (or small group). Second, it's conversation based which is exactly what college-age people want. So, it's not a curriculum drenched in information that will turn off a younger person and yet it provides some structure for older adults—which they tend to prefer.

College Ministry from Scratch

A Practical Guide to Start and Sustain a Successful College Ministry

by Chuck Bomar

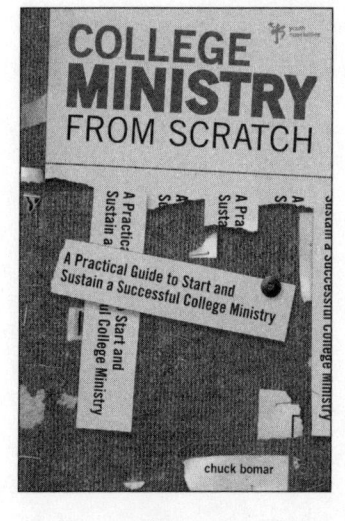

Written by college ministry expert, Chuck Bomar, *College Ministry from Scratch* provides simple tips and practical ideas for anyone looking to start something for college-age people in their congregation.

Keeping in mind that a youth worker or volunteer launching a college ministry already leads a busy life, this book is easy to digest and offers insights on everything from leading overseas mission trips or winter retreats to leading a small group or Sunday school class. This handy resource addresses the simple, but often intimidating task of initiating meetings with students, and even offers a list of questions they can ask when having coffee with a student. Organized by topic, it's an easy book for leaders to jump in and out of, as they need it, and is sure to help any size church begin to meet the needs of the college-age people in their congregation.

Softcover: 978-0-310-67105-3

Available in stores and online!

College Ministry 101

A Guide to Working with 18-25 Year Olds

by Chuck Bomar

Eighteen- to 25-year-olds, more than anyone else, are trying to find their place in society. But during this crucial time period they are also living through an array of experiences that force them to reevaluate their beliefs and assumptions. As a result, many students disconnect from the church after high school.

College Ministry 101 will help you understand the college-age-stage in order to better minister to students' needs. This book will provide leaders with practical ministry philosophies about how to effectively minister to college students through mentor relationships, what students need in their day-to-day lives, how to work with volunteers in college ministry, and how to turn college-age students into genuine disciples.

Softcover: 978-0-310-28547-2

Available in stores and online!

Share Your Thoughts

With the Author: Your comments will be forwarded to the author when you send them to *zauthor@zondervan.com*.

With Zondervan: Submit your review of this book by writing to *zreview@zondervan.com*.

Free Online Resources at

www.zondervan.com

Zondervan AuthorTracker: Be notified whenever your favorite authors publish new books, go on tour, or post an update about what's happening in their lives at www.zondervan.com/authortracker.

Daily Bible Verses and Devotions: Enrich your life with daily Bible verses or devotions that help you start every morning focused on God. Visit www.zondervan.com/newsletters.

Free Email Publications: Sign up for newsletters on Christian living, academic resources, church ministry, fiction, children's resources, and more. Visit www.zondervan.com/newsletters.

Zondervan Bible Search: Find and compare Bible passages in a variety of translations at www.zondervanbiblesearch.com.

Other Benefits: Register yourself to receive online benefits like coupons and special offers, or to participate in research.